EXTRAORDINARY PRAISE FOR

Feminasty

"Erin Gibson—one-half of the crazy-popular *Throwing Shade* podcast—is as sharply funny as she is unabashedly feminist. Damn smart, too. Each of the essays in this book is an eye-opening lesson in how the patriarchy is working against us, and how to fight back. #themoreyouknow"

—*Cosmopolitan*

"Erin Gibson is well versed in the art of couching awful news in humor. The same goes for her new book, in which she mercilessly takes that skill to the next level. FEMINASTY is cathartic, hilarious, enlightening, and rage provoking."

—*Glamour*

"Gibson blazes across the page like a firework shooting over a landscape of ALL CAPS and italics for emphasis...FEMINASTY is a Best-Friend Book. Reading it feels like having a feminist hype-woman in your corner. She's taking patriarchal bullies apart with the catty, flippant venom they deserve. She's pouring you a glass of something bubbly. She's making you laugh till it runs out your nose."

—*Portland Mercury*

"We dare you to find a more relatable book title. Comedian and *Throwing Shade* podcast host Erin Gibson gave us the gift of this collection of omg-I'm-literally-dying

level hilarious essays that tackle the 'hidden rules that make life as a woman harder.' Not only will you learn sh*t, but you'll also laugh a lot. What could be better than that?" —Betches.com

"FEMINASTY is laugh-out-loud funny. But it'll also make you seriously mad. Erin Gibson, cohost of the podcast *Throwing Shade*, sheds light on niche women's issues that aren't at the forefront of the news but desperately need our attention." —HelloGiggles.com

"It feels like you're chatting with your wittier and much funnier best friend." —*Citizen Times*

"Gibson uses her very presence as an act of defiance— she's a loud Southern lady with size-11 feet who grew up poor white trash—and readers will be grateful that she can't keep her mouth shut." —*Booklist*

"The rhetorical purposes of the work are clear: Gibson seeks to lift up women at every opportunity, especially by changing the gender balance in political power." —*Kirkus Reviews*

"In her edgy, fierce, and funny debut essay collection, co-median and *Throwing Shade* podcast cohost Gibson serves up scathing wit and graphic observations on the 'insane ways people try to control' women... The result is a bubbly acid bath of clever invective encouraging her fellow women to make the world a better place." —*Publishers Weekly*

Feminasty

The Complicated Woman's Guide to
Surviving the Patriarchy without
Drinking Herself to Death

Erin Gibson

GRAND CENTRAL
PUBLISHING

NEW YORK   BOSTON

Grand Central Publishing
Hachette Book Group
1290 Avenue of the Americas, New York, NY 10104
grandcentralpublishing.com
twitter.com/grandcentralpub

Originally published in hardcover and ebook by Grand Central Publishing in September 2018.

First Trade Edition: October 2019

Grand Central Publishing is a division of Hachette Book Group, Inc. The Grand Central Publishing name and logo is a trademark of Hachette Book Group, Inc.

The publisher is not responsible for websites (or their content) that are not owned by the publisher.

The Hachette Speakers Bureau provides a wide range of authors for speaking events. To find out more, go to www.hachettespeakersbureau.com or call (866) 376-6591.

Book design by Marie Mundaca

Library of Congress Control Number: 2018946511

ISBNs: 978-1-4555-7187-1 (trade pbk.), 978-1-4555-7188-8 (ebook)

Printed in the United States of America

LSC-C

10 9 8 7 6 5 4 3 2 1

To women.
You are not my competition.

INTRODUCTION

During the Great Depression, Lysol was the number one form of contraception for women. You read that correctly. Lysol, the number one product for cleaning up elementary school puke, was marketed back then as a feminine hygiene douche for women. "Feminine hygiene" in the early 1930s wasn't about keeping your flapper hoo-ha fresh and minty; it was woman code for "birth control," which was illegal.[1] So Lysol stepped in and became a woman's first and only resort to prevent pregnancy.

While the days of disinfectant douches are behind us—because we are too young to have experienced

---

1 It wasn't until 1938 before married women were allowed to buy diaphragms without being jailed—and single women would have to wait until 1972 to get birth control, the same year email was invented.

it or because it melted our insides and we died—women still have about four hundred million obstacles to overcome. Some we know about—unequal pay, under-representation in government, reproductive restrictions, lack of floor-length mirrors in hotel rooms—but a lot of them are harder to identify. They're the white noise of oppression that we've accepted as lady business as usual, and the patriarchy wants to keep it that way.

Too bad I don't give a fuck about what the patriarchy wants.

I'm here to make sure we're smarter than the patriarchy. That we identify every single way they're trying to fuck with our lives. That we see through their lies and deceit and power-hungry motivations and find ways to subvert and destroy their system.[2]

It's time to go HAM on the patriarchy. And I'm just the bitch to show you how.

For the last nine years, I've dedicated my career to repackaging lady sadness into digestible comedy so that we can all be a little smarter and a little savvier and can laugh together at the insane ways people try to control us. For the past seven years, I've been the cohost of the absurdist political comedy podcast *Throwing Shade*, where I've been talking

---

2   Except for In-N-Out. They can stay.

shit about Mike Pence since he was just a small-time rat-eyed worm man/governor of Indiana. The time I've spent reading about his antichoice state legislation is more than I've invested in getting my brows waxed, and I am *very* punctual with my facial hair maintenance. On the show, I've covered women's issues, from Catholic hospitals' subpar treatment of black mothers to female students being kicked out of proms for wearing suits to the WNBA pay gap. *Throwing Shade* wasn't my first job verbally eviscerating the worst of the worst. As a political writer/director at Funny or Die, Michele Bachmann, Megyn Kelly, Michelle Duggar, Jan Brewer, Mitt and Ann Romney, and the entire state of Utah made making fun of them too easy. But I truly owe my career to my first job in political comedy. As the host of "Modern Lady," a segment on the TV show *InfoMania*, I researched the shitty trends of women in the media, like female cops all being victims of a crime or celebrity breastfeeding shaming, and made them funny. Or tried to at least. You've never seen my "An Independent Girl's Guide to Valentine's Day" segment and you never will.

My transformation into a childless, career-obsessed, nail-biting, hell-bent feminist she-devil banshee was not easy or fast. It took me twenty years of soul-crushing defeats completely tied to my gender. When I was eight years old and standing a cool adult height of five foot nine in the third grade, I was a loveable, joy-filled dork who found the inner confidence to rock pink geometric Garfield glasses AND size 10 (adult) hot-pink Reebok high-tops. As a kid, I had my head in the clouds, dreaming of being the next Steven Spielberg. Dreams that were effortlessly crushed by teachers who didn't have the imagination to consider a woman just as capable of standing behind a camera and bossing people around while the director of photography does all the work.

In junior high, having never grown into my massive feet, I tried to be "acceptably cool," not "the way I want to be cool, cool" by getting contact lenses, which allowed me to see that even without glasses, I was still a gangly geek with a bad home perm who played the clarinet and wore paisley MC Hammer pants. I was made fun of, had chronic nosebleeds, and was known for farting as I tripped up the gym bleachers. Shitty preteens made fun of my nose hairs, told me I was ugly, and one seventh-grade boy threatened to murder me in science class once a week in graphic detail. My sister was also having a hard time, so we held our own school dances in the yard space under our A-frame's deck, and a trickling of other white trash children would wander over after WrestleMania to eat pigs in a blanket and dance to C+C Music Factory.

I stumbled through high school an unfuckable

dork, and in college I blossomed into a functional alcoholic with a sporadic sex life and a complicated eating disorder that involved taking daily double doses of appetite suppressants, drinking Starbucks venti vanilla lattes, and smoking more cigarettes than Humphrey Bogart and Kristen Stewart combined. I wanted to go to college to study photography but was scared people would think I was weird (I was weird; I *am* weird), so I got a useless marketing degree.

I was on a very specific life track. A track that ensured I would marry the first guy who was nice enough to hold my chunky highlighted hair as I vomited spaghetti and vodka into my Nine West pumps in front of the dumpster behind Club Europa. Then we'd have three terrible children, all of them different combinations of the worst things about both of us. He'd have the NERVE to divorce ME at forty-five, and I'd be relegated to taking my kids to soccer practice wearing oversized T-shirts printed with things like "I Gave Him the Skinniest Years of My Life" while watching him and his new girlfriend, a twenty-five-year-old Toyota repair shop receptionist named Mollee, feed each other corn dogs in the bleachers.

But before I headed down that path, my Feminist Jesus carried me on the beach of life just when I needed her. Tria Wood, a fierce, independent feminist, came into my life and set me on another road. She gave me a copy of Susan Faludi's *Backlash*, which I read in three days.[3] The book unraveled the suppressive gender sweater I'd been sweating in my whole life. I stopped hating myself and other women and redirected my rage at the dumbass, cis straight white men in authority who were ruining my life with their power, religion, wealth, and sex eyes. I started figuring out who I wanted to be and erasing the person I *thought* people wanted me to be. I came up with a really good personality for myself— a charming, funny bitch who wants to destroy the status quo by any means necessary…as long as *RuPaul's Drag Race* is not on. A powerful alpha female who will figuratively stick her high heels in the patriarchy's nutsack while eating a slice of margherita pizza. An unapologetic cunt who corrects any dude who thinks she gives a shit about his stupid, uninformed, unsolicited opinion. A feminasty.

---

3   Which is fast for me. *Are You There God? It's Me, Margaret* took me three weeks.

THE TERRIFYING PROSPECT OF MIKE "VAGINAS ARE THE DEVIL'S MOUTH FLAPS" PENCE

When I was ten years old, all I wanted to do was listen to Def Leppard, marry Doogie Howser, and be old enough to smoke cigarettes. We had just moved to Ironton, Ohio, from Texas, and I had no friends. My favorite thing to do was take pictures of my baby dolls in dangerous situations like hanging them by one toe from an elm tree or placing their head under a car wheel. I was a busy child auteur living in my own bubble world, and the last place I wanted to be wasting my creative time was Sunday morning at Catholic church, listening as a priest made the story of a man with incredible powers mind-numbingly boring.

The only exciting thing that ever happened in church was being filled with absolute jealousy at all those braggers who got to take Communion.

Not me. I wasn't in the Cracker of Christ Club. I wanted watered-down grape juice and paperlike crackers (because I was hungry), but I wasn't allowed bland early St. Lawrence brunch because my mom didn't let me take catechism classes. We went out of a sense of duty and ritual, but there was something holding my mom back from leaving me there to learn from those people. She is justifiably scarred having gone to Catholic school, along with her ten brothers and sisters, until one of the nuns hit my uncle Freddy and my grandpa pulled them out temporarily. Sister Clematis, known in my family as "Pennywise in a habit," would take a wooden ruler and slam it on my six-year-old mother's tiny little lady hands for coloring outside the lines. Chew on a pencil? Get nun-slapped in the back of the head. Be restless in your chair, and she would give you a warm hug and tell you it's going to be okay. Just kidding, she would sneak up behind you and rattle your chair like a hurricane.

Father Frailey drove a Corvette, which he parked by the children's playground and then would go ape if their kickballs bounced into his holy muscle car. And I'd be filled with regret if I didn't mention Monsignor York's yearly all-boys trip to Myrtle Beach. Just an innocent romp to a beach city Coed.com named the number twelve "trashiest spring break destination" in 2016. But we still went to church, taking all that into consideration and whatever else my family doesn't talk about, because that's what you did. My grandmother Norma Bell was a devout Catholic, having converted to marry my grandfather, who was a first-generation Irish Catholic street rat.[1] Norma Bell was raised Southern Baptist, and they let it be known with death threats that they didn't approve of her jumping onto ship Catholic.[2] Slowly, over a long period of time, my family stopped putting up with the church bullshit. They woke up from the spell and Kool-Aid Man–ed through the buttressed walls, running backward, middle fingers up. I owe the Catholic Church a lot. If they hadn't been absolutely terrible to my family, I would have never developed a mafia-like hatred for them. You mess with my family, Pope, you mess with me…an adult woman who is always showing up at birthday parties dressed in the same clothes as the toddlers.

Who I dislike more than the church are the religious posers who take the parables of the Bible and use them as a weapon to hurt and control women. They're like a Christian mullet—religion in the

---

1 I am third-generation Irish street rat and if you want proof, look at my ears and my hair when it dries naturally. I look like an extra in *Once*.
2 To me, the only difference between Southern Baptist and Catholicism is the variations in their racism.

front, evil in the back.[3] Well, I'm not fucking standing for this hypocritical behavior. Not from Christian minister and GOP superstar Mike Huckabee, who went on Fox News and compared women's health clinic Planned Parenthood to a heroin dealer. I'm not taking it from Wisconsin state assembly GOP rep and Catholic Roger Rivard, who said, "Some girls, they rape so easy." And I'm definitely not taking it from king religious ding-dong, husband to "Mother," and analog phone enthusiast Mike Pence. Mike Pence, the forty-eighth vice president[4] of the United States, is someone I am very worried might become the most powerful man in the Western world. There's a lot of pressure to get Donald Trump out of the White House, but the man who would then be president is much worse. Trump can at least be tricked into doing sort of the right thing for a day, but Pence has been applying his steadfast religious anti-women dogma since 1999.

Mike Pence started sharing his moral oppression of females in the late '90s, tackling one of the

---

3   I'm not saying all Christians are assholes. There are certainly good ones out there. Maybe you're a good person and you also happen to believe that a virgin can give birth. I can accept that. I think that plants will share the secrets of the universe if I touch them while I'm on DMT. We all believe weird stuff.

4   Some presidents had two vice presidents and some vice presidents served under two presidents and so now the math is all fucked up and seriously messing with my need for symmetry.

biggest threats to his worldview—Disney's *Mulan*.[5] Maybe you haven't seen it—because you're busy searching for pictures of baby animal enemies falling asleep holding each other—so let me explain the plot. The movie's about a young woman who pretends to be her father in order to enlist in the Chinese army. When they find out she's a woman, they spare her life even though it's a crime punishable by death. She later sneaks into the emperor's palace, disguised as a concubine, and rescues everyone. Mike Pence wasn't upset about the implied sex slavery or executions. No, he felt the movie would radicalize women into thinking they could serve in combat, which was not permitted at that time.[6] Just to be clear, he was so mad after seeing A CARTOON GIRL BECOME A WAR HERO, he opened up Word '97 and started typing a diatribe that even paper clip helper Clippy was like, "Are you sure you want to type this ridiculous shit?" When he was done, he posted it on the website for his radio show, *The Mike Pence Show*. Or let's be real, someone else uploaded it to his website. I believe Mike Pence knows HTML like I believe Johnny Depp volunteers at a women's shelter. While Pence

---

5   Unearthed by Andrew Kaczynski for BuzzFeed, who deserves a
     medal for finding it.
6   It wasn't until 2013 that the *Mulan* propaganda finally infiltrated
     the secretary of defense.

set out to air his opposition to women serving in combat, he took the opportunity to say that women shouldn't be in the military at all. He wrote:

> The hard truth of our experiment with gender integration is that is has been an almost complete disaster for the military and for many of the individual women involved.

An adult man, triggered by a Disney movie.[7] This children's entertainment is a threat to our military system and he's the only patriot red, white, and blue enough to say it! On the outside he's a red, white, and blue patriot who thinks women are precious porcelain dolls Jesus gift-wrapped for men to impregnate while we Clorox shower tiles, but on the inside he's scared of us. And he doesn't want us to have guns in the Sunni Triangle because we might discover the real enemy is our country. Or he's scared that little girls might grow up to feel that they are capable of doing anything a man can do. Whatever he's afraid of, he's afraid, and he might make you believe this outrage-wrapped fear is justified by referencing in his piece that women are sexually assaulted in the military. He specifically references

---

7   That wasn't full of consent issues like *Sleeping Beauty*.

what he calls the "Tailhook scandal," which is, according to him, an incident "involving scores of high ranking navy fighter pilots who molested subordinate women." For the purposes of this chapter, I'd love to use different language that paints a clearer picture of what Tailhook was. I'd like to refer to it as "the Ultimate Gang Rape at Tailhook, a living hellscape where eighty-three women and seven men were sexually assaulted by more than one hundred officers." Pence is afraid that *Mulan* will send a message to little girls—you won't get raped in the American military—and he knows that's not true. Mike Pence could have used *Mulan* as a paradigm for what the U.S. military could be, where women are treated with respect and not just reiterated the un-Jesus-like way the military actually treats women (and men). Take rape out of the equation and Mike Pence still thinks women have no business in the military. He type screams:

> Housing, in close quarters, young men and women (in some cases married to non-military personnel) at the height of their physical and sexual potential is the height of stupidity.

Don't you picture him saying this while chugging an A&W root beer on the back of a plugged-in golf cart, parked in the middle of his garage, surrounded by unused tools and his pals, four old white guys wearing varying translations of blue polos. The kind of guys who excuse themselves to fart outside but still cover it up with a too-loud cough just in case.

"Guys, you know how children's cartoons get you thinking about how sexually explosive eighteen-year-old soldiers are?"

"Uh, yeah, sure, Mike?"

Confused looks all around. Kip Tupper, real estate mogul and prayer buddy, snaps off a bite of celery and swallows it aggressively. This might be a loooong night.

I know Mike Pence because Mike Pence is every dad I grew up around in Texas. My friend Avery's dad used to drink Natural Light with us in his garage and talk about how women shouldn't be cops—well, his exact words were "I hate bitch cops"—and then make a hard left turn into some Rain Man–like regurgitation of pages of Scripture. The experience is like enjoying the whimsy of the It's a Small World ride one second, and then the next you're in a whiskey barrel about to go over Niagara Falls.

Think Mike Pence is only focused on destroying the lives of men and women "at the height of their physical and sexual potential"? He's also given your grandma a nice one-two punch in the crotch when he tried to pay for Katrina relief by cutting Medicare. Yes, he cut the budget that assists the old mothers and fathers we should be honoring in order to pay for the blessed poor because the Bible has all those passages about "thou shalt never cut the warmongering budget to help the helpless." Either group he chooses not to help, he's hurting the good Christians. Like the best Christian who ever lived, my grandma Norma Bell Thompson. She wore a rosary, prayed before every meal, never missed Mass, and gave money she couldn't afford to give to the church. She made me biscuits and gravy even when it was clear I was getting fat. She laughed when I cussed. She took in homeless people. And she loved everyone exactly the same. When I was ten, sitting on Grandma's porch reading *Bridge to Terabithia*, again, while my cousin Stephanie and her Filipino boyfriend made out, a neighbor walked by and abruptly directed a racial slur toward Stephanie's boyfriend, and my grandma came flying out the screen door and went HAM on that guy. She was screaming, "Jesus doesn't discriminate in this house!" Mike Pence could learn a lesson from Norma Thompson! If someone told my grandma they were gay, she would hold them and squeeze them into her DD boobs and tell them they were loved. She wouldn't do everything in her power to destroy them using the Bible as her weapon. As governor of Indiana, Mike Pence diverted funds from the state's Ryan White CARE Act—the largest federally funded program to assist people living with HIV/AIDS—and put that money into conversion-therapy facilities.[8] At best, conversion therapy is like going to a camp for a week where adults yell at you to force you to be straight; at worst, it's like going to a camp for a week where adults yell and hit you to force you to be straight. It doesn't fucking work at changing someone's sexual orientation, and the American Medical Association and the American Psychological Association both agree it's awful. Both oppose conversion therapy because it's attempting to fix something that's not wrong, oftentimes using psychologically and sometimes physically violent methods.

Only twelve states in the United States ban conversion therapy, and Mike Pence's state is not one of them. Neither does Louisiana, a state that housed a legal conversion camp that took one of my best friends away. During college, I was working at America's finest chino retailer, Gap. The floor manager found out very quickly that my perfectionist anxiety was uniquely suited for the fitting room, and that's where I stayed for two years, stuck in a windowless hallway, repeating the same greetings and folding

---

8   After he waited two months to respond to the worst per capita HIV outbreak in U.S. history, Pence said he'd "pray on" if he would send Scott County clean needles. No word on how GOD HIMSELF RESPONDED.

the reasonably priced separates again. Most of the people who worked with me were high school kids who only had the job because they were bored. They would stand in my three-by-four-foot work box and refuse to put back clothes. But then there was Hope. She was a twenty-five-year-old social worker from a small town in Louisiana who worked at the Gap for extra money. She was loud and sweet and loved to put people in their place. She called everyone "baby-doll" and when she came into my glorified closet, it was for jokes and to help. We were inseparable. After work on Saturdays, we'd get drunk at P.F. Chang's, go to the gay clubs, smoke a ton of cigarettes, then get up on Sunday and watch *Meet the Press*. One night, she took me out for a non-PFC Chinese dinner and nervously blurted out to me that she was a lesbian. I don't think she expected me to squeal with joy, and then squeal even louder when she told me she'd been dating our queer hairdresser. I was so excited for both of them! When the three of us would go out, I could feel how happy they both were. And bonus, since Hope was hotter than me, it meant way more dick for me. Everyone wins!!! Then out of nowhere, Hope disappeared. I didn't know where she was; her girlfriend hadn't heard from her in days. Neither of us knew her parents, and she never really talked about them much, so we couldn't call them. Then one day, she emailed to tell us her parents had come to "rescue" her and put her in a place with people who could help her "figure things out." Her email read like a letter from someone sucked into a cult.

"I'm safe here with the Branch Davidians. David may be a megalomaniac who thinks he's Jesus, but don't worry, there are also plenty of guns."

She said she wasn't a lesbian anymore, she was never a lesbian, just confused. I never heard from Hope again. I've lost her email since I abandoned Adidas69@hotmail.com, an address I hope a Korn fan is putting to good use. Wherever Hope is, I hope she's okay. These Christian conversion centers are not only dangerous, but also when you're put there by your family, you have very few options of finding someone to help you escape them, which is why they should be illegal. Because honestly, what's worse in the eyes of the Lord—bringing a snake to Mardi Gras, which is *illegal* in Louisiana, or forcing a teenager to watch lesbian porn and then hitting her whenever two women have sex, which is *legal* in Louisiana?

When he's not busy voting against the minimum wage, making low-level offenders stay in jail forever, or defunding Syrian refugee rescue groups in his state, Pence is using his impenetrable armor of religion to roll back reproductive rights. He's tried to redefine rape as "forcible" or "not forcible"; he's signed laws to shut down abortion clinics; he's encouraged women with nonviable pregnancies to carry them to term, and, the worst of the worst, he's forced women to pay for the burial of fetal remains after abortion procedures or after she has a miscarriage.

"And on the seventh day, Christ rose and told a grieving woman to wipe her tears and fork over $1,500 for the burial costs."

You're probably thinking, *How does Mike Pence find the time to hate so many different kinds of women and keep his skin looking so young?* I have it on good authority he ritualistically sneaks into prison births to soak his skin in newborn vernix while watching the mother shackled to her hospital bed. It's the only thing keeping that turkey neck in check. His nastiness comes directly from the edicts of the Evangelical Church, which he joined in college. According to an election piece the *New York Times* did on Pence, he was enamored with one of his frat brothers' gold cross necklaces when his brother said to him, "Remember, Mike, you have got to wear it in your heart before you wear it around your neck." And then he was at a Christian music festival in Kentucky, which we'll go ahead and call Godchella, where he "gave [his] life to Jesus Christ." So, Mike Pence found extreme Christianity because of a shiny necklace and shrooms.

According to a study by the Public Religion Research Institute, white Evangelical Christians, compared to other religious groups, think they are more persecuted than any other sect[9], which is supremely delusional considering they are dictating the terms of American politics. Mike Pence makes laws that hurt other people because he feels his faith is under attack. Because in his Christian worldview, the freedom of women and minorities and LGBTQI people is an attack on Christianity, so he has to be a bad Christian to protect his Christian life of being a nice person. If he's a true Christian, in the purest sense of the idea, he'd downsize from his state-subsidized Tudor-style home filled with silk shantung armchairs into a modest home or at the very least, give his BUTLER, which the state of Indiana pays for, a day off. But the reality is, Mike Pence and his wife Karen's freedoms aren't under attack. Their way of life is not threatened. The truth is, they don't have many problems. Karen has so few problems in her life, she has to make them up. Which is why she invented "That's My Towel!" towel charm. Karen is concerned with so many things—the death of babies at abortion facto-

---

9   At the 2017 World Summit, Pence told the audience, "No people today face greater hostility than followers of Christ." Yeah? Say that to a Scientologist. Can you imagine standing in front of the whole world, serving head-to-toe Men's Warehouse off-the-rack realness, talking utter horseshit about Operating Thetan levels and engrams?

ries, gay people marrying—but she's focused much of her time on this absolutely relatable global crisis. On her website, she writes:

> I have had so many times where I was swimming at a friend's beach house, pool, or lake house, using their matching beautiful beach towels. Lo and behold, I would go in the water for a dip or up to the house for a beverage, and when I came back to my towel, it was gone! Someone else had grabbed my towel unknowingly…because all of the towels looked the same.

A problem everyone can relate to! I have SO MANY friends who own second properties near water and I can't even keep up with my friends who have a POOL AT THEIR HOME. God, I must know thousands. And all of my very busy women friends can always find the time to buy EXTRA MATCHING towels just for the pool. So thank goodness Karen has solved a massive problem that exists for so few rich people by inventing a tiny fucking charm you stab into your towel so that Trisha's son can stop fucking using yours. They look like what you'd imagine, tiny sailboats and seagulls and sunglasses. JUST KIDDING! They're shaped like french fries, cameras, and trains! I bet if Karen were on Christian Mingle, she'd have those listed under her interests. "Hi, I'm Karen, Christian fanatic who loves the finest things in life—cameras, french fries, and trains. Looking for strong Joseph type with an aversion to the poor and a passion for the Christ. Get it! LOL! P.S. I love to LOL!"

Mike Pence is not a Christian. He is a religious terrorist who now has a lot of power to do a lot of terrible things to people in this country who need a helping hand from a Good Christian. If Jesus were alive today, first of all, he would look exactly like the beardiest version of the Avett Brothers, and secondly, if he were the leper-loving, bread-multiplying, poor-serving saint the Bible claims he was, he would have some strong words and disappointing head shakes for Mike Pence as he tells him, "You're not welcome in my faith, you piece of shit." Impeaching Trump is not the answer, because the next bozo in line is a guy who thinks *The Handmaid's Tale* is a wish-fulfillment fantasy, like *Field of Dreams*, but with more state-sanctioned rape. We wait out their term, helping women who are in the crosshairs of their villain-ous laws. Then, we flush them out with a tsunami of overqualified women who won't forget what they did to us. These men will never dry off, no matter how many be-charmed towels Karen Pence hands them.

HOW TO EXPLAIN #METOO TO THE DUMMIES WHO DON'T GET IT

The year 2017 was shit. No, it was worse than shit. It was taking a shit in a porta-potty at a food festival while a forklift turns it upside down. It was doused in gallons of Kogi taco diarrhea, forcefully expelled cheese curds, and pad thai soft stool, then sent to an un-air-conditioned storage facility in the Antelope Valley on an unseasonably hot day. Open the door and take a whiff: That was 2017. Caked-on human shit smothered in throw-up, fermented to perfection. It was a year of constant nuclear war threats, government shutdowns, and a stock market more erratic than Shia LaBeouf's performance-art manifesto.

But despite the rank BM that is our political reality, some really amazing things happened for women. *Wonder Woman* was the highest-grossing movie by a female director ever, I was able to find a pair of jeans that didn't suffocate my labia,[1] and Tarana Burke's #MeToo movement woke people up to the novel idea that female bodies aren't jungle gyms for pervs. The toppling of the patriarchy was in full swing. Sure it was going on against a backdrop of imminent nuclear war—but it was happening! The problem is, amid the celebratory "My rape kit is being processed!" brunches and "I got my handsy boss fired after ten years!" bar parties, we didn't stop to think about what we stand to lose…according to people who never wanted #MeToo to happen.

Here's what they won't shut up about:

1. #METOO IS RUINING MASCULINITY!

No one believes this harder than Fox News online scribe and circus pony Suzanne Venker. It is an understatement to say Suzanne dislikes feminism, considering she writes articles titled "Is Equality Ruining Your Marriage?" and the right-to-the-point "Society Is Creating a New Crop of Alpha Women Who Are Unable to Love." A better way to put it might be "Suzanne Venker wishes she could

---

1 There's mesh netting making up the crotch and my labia can hang loose, like two little worms in an upside-down convertible.

Single White Female[2] feminism right in the eye with a stiletto."

Suzanne is passionate about a lot of things—chunky bright necklaces,[3] cropped Spanish-teacher haircuts, and destroying the slow progress feminists have made because they've ruined her 1950s nuclear family fever dream. If we had it Suzanne's way, women would still be spending their days revacuuming the same spot in the living room while wearing cone bras. You know, like malfunctioning fembots. The only feminist thing Suzanne has ever done is watch *Leave It to Beaver*, and I'm sure the double entendre escaped her. Side note: If you're a woman running for office, I'd like to encourage you to use "Leave It to Beaver" as your campaign slogan.

"You want a candidate for change? Leave it to beaver!"

It should come as no surprise, then, that Suzanne was pissed about #MeToo. So she did what she does

---

2   I want to do a remake of this movie where Allie (Bridget Fonda) meets a wonderful black woman, Asha, who is also looking for a roommate, but whom Allie ultimately doesn't offer the room to because she's black. Allie meets soon-to-be-psycho Hendra (Jennifer Jason Leigh), who ticks off all her race requirements. Three weeks later, police find Allie's charred body in the furnace—and guess who rents her second-floor walk-up in the Upper West Side? That's right: Asha.

3   This is the first of many references to chunky necklaces. They are mostly worn by terrible women who think their vaguely ethnic colorful heavy neck décor is a personality. Mentioning them is part of my brand. Get into it.

best—slamming her French-manicured tips onto her Dell desktop, pressing send on her Juno.net email and releasing a scathing anti-#MeToo piece to whatever Jabba the Hutt look-alike runs Fox News these days. In keeping with her "saying it all with the title" naming technique, she called it, "#MeToo Isn't About Sexual Harassment, It's About Destroying Masculinity."

Like any other Pulitzer-worthy reporter, Suzanne is kind enough to explain the #MeToo movement in terms her audience will understand:

> But grievances are like crabgrass: The more heat they get, the more it spreads.[4]

Crabgrass. It's the perfect analogy for readers whose number-one life problem is lawn aeration. What I like about this analogy is that it uses a logic applying to lots of stuff besides crabgrass—the thing about grievances is they're a lot like Toll House cookie dough; the more heat they get, the more they spread.

---

4 Sorry, grammar addicts, this is how she writes—from the heart, not from the rules. I'm lucky to have an editor and a copy editor and a writer's assistant who don't allow the world to see how my Southern education turned my eyes and brains grammar blind. I would also like to shout-out my third-grade teacher for making me diagram sentences in front of the class while I was hysterically crying because I didn't understand grammatical structure instead of taking me aside and helping me understand. I do hope she is dead.

She goes on to say:

The current outcry against men in power has nothing to do with giving a voice to victims. It's about putting feminists in power. What would feminists do with this power? Destroy all that is left of men and masculinity, among other things.

Among what other things? I don't have time for other things—I'm chockablock dropping men off on Lord of the Flies Island. In all seriousness, I tell my husband, Ale, when the feminist revolution comes, I will visit him on Man Island, one to two times a year, and it won't be all bad—think about all the pals he can talk about Bitcoin with.

Suzanne doesn't lay out how we'll get this immense power or when it will come to us, but I really want to know. Like will we get a card in the mail or a phone call? Is it like Publishers Clearing House? Will a group of people in suits with balloons ring our doorbell and tell us we have it? Suzanne doesn't seem to have the slightest idea what feminists will do to get this power, but she knows one thing for certain:

At the end of the day, what feminists want is a whole new America. And they will band together until they get it.

I don't need a whole new America. Okay, yeah, it would be nice to live in a world where men don't graze my butt on their way to grab the thirty-five-pound free weights, but I want to keep some parts of America—weed lemonade, Miss Vanjie, interesting ankle boots, and Maxine Waters—exactly as they are. What Suzanne means by "a whole new America" is an America where the rules are different. Where the rules are female. Which panics her. What would Suzanne do when we've feminized the system and we eliminate homelessness, run the banks—that don't fail—and institute massive tax write-offs for waxing, highlights, and BB creme, all while requiring a mandatory three days off for periods, building a system of childcare providers, and outlawing fringe jackets on men with ponytails? Suzanne is probably the type of person who had a nervous breakdown when Mastercard changed its logo. She can't handle a new world order. Even one that benefits her.

2. #METOO IS DEVASTATING SEXY HOLLYWOOD MOVIES!

The *Hollywood Reporter*'s Tatiana Siegel is another woman bravely standing up on behalf of the status quo. In her article "How the #MeToo Movement Could Kill Some Sexy Hollywood Movies," she argues that the third installment of *Fifty Shades of Grey* may be its last thanks to #MeToo. Now, I've seen the first *Fifty Shades of Grey* and let me tell you, it's a joke to call it erotica. I get that *Fifty Shades* author E.L. Fudge wets her Hanes panties at the theory of an emotionally broken Christian Grey coming at her in his dumpy Tommy Hilfiger jeans. But, IM(notsoH)O, if my options were to either let the Hilfiger jeans guy jerk me off with a horse whip OR be cursed to live as a chain wallet belonging to the lead singer of a Christian rock band for the rest of my life, I would choose the latter. If the #MeToo movement means women's boundaries are respected AND I never have to see a *Fifty Shades* poster on a bus stop again, it's collateral damage I can get behind. The *Fifty Shades* movie franchise needs to make like a cum tissue and be flushed down the toilet. Or, like what happens in my house, get eaten by my dog. (Don't worry, I always fish it out of his mouth before he swallows it.)

And you'll never guess what other art house films are on the chopping block because of #MeToo. Just look at how Louis C.K.'s hot inter-gen romance, *I Love You, Daddy*, was censored by meanie film distributors just because Louie C.K. jerked off in front of women in the past (back when no one cared), completely ignoring that the movie was, at its core, a heaping piece of old boner intellectualism in the first place. It's not fair! Then there was the Hugh Hefner biopic starring Jared Leto, a movie not going forward even though they did the right thing and fired gloppy fried coconut shrimp buffet Brett Ratner. Isn't it sad we won't get to know what brand of baby oil Hugh Hefner used on his old lizard dick? Thanks a lot #MeToo!

3. #METOO HAS WRECKED LUNCHES WITH MY GRANDPA

I took my grandpa to Red Lobster for his birthday. We were having a nice time, enjoying our Cheddar Bay Biscuits and seahorse-sized shrimps, when he asked me what I thought of the #MeToo movement. I told him it was about making people aware of what kind of abuse women endure and he said, "Well, you should have been there in Korea. People did crazy stuff and everybody was okay with it." Then I said, "Okay, so a commanding officer grabbed your balls and told you if you didn't suck his dick you'd be on latrine duty?" And he said, "No, that would be awful." Then he got quiet and lost himself in his Admiral's Feast. The entire lunch cost me $35 and he learned nothing!

4. #METOO IS ALIENATING OLDER WOMEN

One hundred famous French women signed a letter in *Le Monde* expressing their concern about the #MeToo movement, which used the much more punk French hashtag #ExposeYourPig (#balancetonporc). The letter involved all the famous French Catherines—art critic Catherine Millet, writer Catherine Robbe-Grillet, and '60s ingénue Catherine Deneuve—expressing their various issues with the movement, like that it reeks of Stalinist thought-policing and the antiquated notion that women are babies who need protecting. The Catherines saw the Grand Canyon–sized chasm between second-wave feminists and younger women who'd simply prefer not to have male coworkers touch their ass creases while they're standing over the copy machine and added a moat. (Also, CAN YOU BELIEVE WE STILL USE COPY MACHINES! WHY?) Here's what I'd like to say to that generation of women: "Shhhhh, it's okay now. You don't have to put up with it. Put on your patent leather white go-go boots and kick them square into the nuts of the old men who were awful to you. We've got your back. And, Deneuve, don't worry about your age— we've got Ryan Murphy now. He's got an imperious opium-addicted swinger club owner role with your name on it."

This line of criticism is also animating the debate stateside. It seasons Daphne Merkin's *New York Times* opinion piece, "Publicly, We Say #MeToo. Privately, We Have Misgivings."

Daphne's general thesis is #MeToo is getting OUT OF CONTROL and I knew I was going to hate this piece after reading the first sentence:

> You can be sure that this weekend at the Golden Globes, Hollywood celebrities, not exactly known for their independent thinking, will turn the red carpet into a #MeToo moment replete with designer duds.

Cool start to a piece, making your case by insulting an entire category of women. I've had the PLEASURE of working with some amazing actresses who are way smarter than me. Sure, there are ding-dongs here and there, but isn't that true of any profession? I worked with a guy at the Gap who was doomed to work the floor because he wasn't smart enough to work the cash register, a machine where the keys' functions were labeled explicitly. Want to process a return? Push the "return" button. Dude couldn't handle it. If you're going to shit on famous people for being sheeple, stick to reality stars. Except Lisa Vanderpump. And Erika Jayne.

Daphne, a time traveler from the year 2050, when

men have become enslaved and are only allowed out of their cages for use as virile sperminators, goes on to make the following assertions in her opinion piece:

- This tactless sense of outrage will sweep up a bunch of innocent men in the process, dooming them to heresy. This aligns with other, even-more-unhinged arguments against #MeToo—like the idea women are wantonly guillotining good guys for the sheer joy of it—which have no basis in reality. Look, if all accusers were really so comfortable outing their perp's dirty laundry, Hollywood and nearly every other industry would cease to exist overnight. I'm surprised there haven't been *more* accusations, is what I'm saying. The idea that this movement has gone too far is like a bag of Lady Doritos: I'm not buyin' it.
- The following passage, wherein she describes the dissonance between the public cheers at another fallen sexual predator and what happens when we're all in private:

> In private it's a different story. "Grow up, this is real life," I hear these same feminist friends say. "What ever happened to flirting?" and "What about the *women* who are the preda-tors?" Some women, including random people I talk to in supermarket lines, have gone so far as to call it an outright witch hunt.

"Excuse me, I know we are just two strangers standing in line to buy cotton candy grapes, but do you think the MeToo movement is a witch hunt?" Also, can we please start using the term "witch hunt" correctly? A witch hunt is when a woman is drowned for her ability to do math.

- She says Garrison Keillor[5] and Al Franken have been victims of trickle-down #MeToo vitriol. We don't want to admit it, but sometimes the lefty males we love who seem to be doing the right thing are actually shitty people, and I don't think a movement should be blamed for reacting to evidence of our friends being assholes.
- Flirting is over. She laments the lack of clarity around what exactly sexual harassment is. She innocently asks, "Is kissing someone in affection, however inappropriately, or showing someone a photo of a nude male torso necessarily predatory behavior?"

The answer to all of that is a (screaming) YES!

Let's use Daphne's examples of what is appro-

---

5 Garrison Keillor's singing voice is of a man who never took "you shouldn't do that" as an answer and I'm not surprised that attitude seeped into his encounters with women. That being said, I do play Garrison's *A Prairie Home Companion* solos from a Bluetooth speaker on my roof to keep coyotes away.

priate flirting to show how predatory it is in this hypothetical playlet:

Steve, the marketing manager, walks into his subordinate Nicole's cubicle.

"Sorry to bother you, Nicole—I know you're working hard on a spreadsheet for today's quarterly marketing meeting, but can you quickly look at this picture of my bare torso and tell me if it's too shiny from lotion?" Then Steve French-kisses her ear.

Here's the question we should be asking—Why does flirting have to be so fucking skeevy? Why can't guys pay compliments to women without any expectations and *then* see what happens? If guys would hit the fucking brakes more often on their *Fast and Furious* flirting tactics, no one would have to guess if the line between what's comfortable and uncomfortable has been crossed.[6]

• The most ignorant sentence in the whole piece is this:

But I don't believe that scattershot, life-destroying denunciations are the way to upend it.

---

6   And guys, if you're thinking of making a SECOND comment about a woman's looks before she responded positively to the first one, maybe go have a glass of water, because BITCH YOU THIRSTY!

Daphne, where were you when these women were having their lives destroyed by these situations? Where was your think piece when they were losing their jobs, their safety? Don't you see all other systems have failed them—that HR managers have ignored their accounts repeatedly for YEARS? Daphne thinks it's our responsibility, not just to defend ourselves, but to make sure the guys who are guilty of sexual assault are protected. The only protection they need now is from women's fists and our weird sharp pointy rings.

- The return of the victim paradigm. This is the most cited reason these women are against #MeToo. The idea that #MeToo is exploiting a new strain of feminism tying being a woman to being a victim—by talking about our assaults, we are shattering the illusion that women are strong as hell. But I see #MeToo exposing the opposite. Every fucking day I see another courageous woman taking to Twitter or Instagram to let us know there's a new asshole on the block. Do you know how fucking brave that is? I see the victimology paradigm not as exposing the crime perpetrated against you but rather believing your only choice is to stay silent.

This is going to sound like a left turn but I assure you it's not. If I lived in a Hudson Valley farmhouse and I demolished a wall and I found some old newspaper in the wall and it was this article and it was dated 1884, I would have said "You go, Daphne!" This piece would have been revolutionary in a time when half the country was still shitting outdoors. But reading it now, it feels like the ideas of an out-of-touch literary snob who doesn't like seeing her elite male friends go down in the fires they started. Daphne is taking her shovel and digging the trench between generations of feminists a little deeper and wider with this piece. There was not one single piece of information on how she thinks men could change their behavior and create fewer problems, only that women are creating more problems. To which I say, ding-dong you're wrong, you stupid bitch.

5. THE #METOO MOVEMENT IS HUMILIATING AZIZ ANSARI

Aziz Ansari, for those of you who don't know, is the star of *Master of None*, wherein he plays an actor navigating his thirties in New York City. First of all, let me say I find it indicative of a comedian's lack of creativity when they get their own TV show and can't come up with another job for them to have on it. Oh, you're a comedian in real life and you're playing a comedian on TV? Revolutionary. Must be why you got into entertainment—to really *expand* your imagination. Look at it this way: Kevin James played a UPS delivery guy. When *Paul Blart: Mall Cop* is finding more inventive ways to package comedic storytelling, maybe try harder, indie comedians.

So, Aziz was called out by a woman who goes by "Grace" for ignoring her nonverbal and verbal boundaries during an evening they spent together. Babe.net, truly the *Paris Review* of feminist clickbait, broke the story in a slapped-together garbage article that did a bad job of handling the nuances of why the story is important.

But even though Babe.net did think it was important to mention exactly what kind of wine Grace ordered before Aziz got handsy, and was super lurid about all the sex moves he used, it was still breathtaking to watch how quickly critics pounced on the piece.

The *Atlantic*'s Caitlin Flanagan said the Ansari hit job only painted women as "angry, temporarily powerful and very very dangerous." Caitlin couldn't wrap her mind around why Grace wouldn't leave if she didn't feel safe, writing, "Apparently there is a whole country full of young women who don't know how to call a cab."

I once slept with a guy on a first date because

he was too drunk to drive me home and I didn't know how to call a cab or even where I was. I'd only been living in Chicago for a few weeks after moving from the suburbs of Houston, where I had learned how to over-pluck my eyebrows but not how to leave uncomfortable sexual scenarios (or that I was even allowed to). And I'm not the only woman I know who has slept with someone because it felt like the only option. (It wasn't all bad, though—he did take me to a really good play about the Holocaust.) "But Erin, what about UBER? What about LYFT?" you scream into the pages. Well, last time I checked, those things still cost money. One time I was stuck at the Addison L station, desperately trying to withdraw cash from my credit card so I could ride the train home. The machine informed me I was maxed out, so for forty-five minutes I speed walked toward my apartment at 3:00 a.m.

Headline News's Ashleigh Banfield said this situation sounded less like sexual assault and more like a bad date and then said more stuff about the story not belonging in the #MeToo movement. Then the reporter behind the story clapped back, calling Ashleigh a "burgundy lipstick, bad highlights, second-wave feminist," which is not cool. We all know the only woman who should be shamed for her highlights is burning-menthol-cigarette-on-a-tanning-bed Jan Brewer. Those are the rules.

Erin Gibson

It's a shame everyone is so focused on the issue of whether or not Grace's experience matters in the landscape of #MeToo, instead of discussing the whole reason Grace came forward. She saw a man participating in a women's movement, who had straight-up ignored her consent. Was she supposed to simply shield her eyes while he swanned down red carpets with a "Time's Up" lapel pin? It makes me furious that women have to experience these things. Which is why I have to take very violent workout classes at least three times a week—kettlebell kick-boxing, yoga for murderers, Pilates 'n' punchin'.

#MeToo is about the myriad ways straight men are failing us—not just by being predators like Harvey Weinstein, but also by ignoring our consent in seemingly smaller ways too. It's about men disregarding our boundaries in intimate situations because they've been taught every dick move is fair in the search for a mate, like we're all just exotic fauna on their hunting safari.

What the people who are so scared of #MeToo need to realize is the goal isn't to limit sex or discourage men from doing their men stuff like MMA and long conversations about Paleo diets. #MeToo is about our complaints being heard for the first time and taken seriously. What some see as the collective anger of a thousand wronged women, I see as the expression of frustration and hurt. #MeToo is about making sure women are not operating out of sheer terror for their own safety. It's about telling the office clown, Chase, it isn't cool or normal to send porn GIFs at the end of Slack convos. We're envisioning a better world, one where Justin Timberlake won't tweet "Here we come!! And DAMN, my wife is hot! #TIMESUP #whywewearblack," sloppily mixing male objectification with a hashtag designed to make people aware of lopsided sexual power dynamics. A new world where Justin Timberlake uses the hashtag #timesup and then ALSO feels shame about starring in Woody Allen's *Wonder Wheel*. A world where Justin Timberlake refuses to do the Super Bowl halftime show WITHOUT Janet Jackson. A world where Justin Timberlake is actually funny and not just a guy in a wig making funny faces.

And in this world, we won't just have the perfect iteration of Justin Timberlake (one who takes a step back once in a while and lets J.C. Chasez shine). Women will feel strong and safe in a world where our boundaries are respected. Also, I promise you, there will be a lot MORE FUCKING! Then, just wait until we move on to the phase where all men are actually taught just how sensitive a clitoris can be or it doesn't make you less of a man to take a finger up the ass. Watch as the whole planet becomes a straight-up safe, consensual fuckfest.

WATCH OUT FOR THESE BACKSTABBING BITCHES

It's 5:30 p.m. and I'm standing outside my sister's bedroom window, my jewel-toned kaleidoscope keyhole unitard drenched with sweat. At some point between before school cigarettes[1] in the parking lot of Cypress Falls High School (GO EAGLES! just kidding, I don't care) and after school drill team dance practice,[2] I've lost my house keys. I'm begging my younger sister, Audrey, to let me in. We're fourteen months apart, Irish

---

1 What can I say? I loved cigarettes. They're the coolest way to get cancer.
2 For those of you not from the South, drill team is a dance group doing a lot of things—funky jazz dances dressed as clowns to "Make 'em Laugh," parent-approved hip-hop to clean EDM, but the main function of the brigade is to perform kick lines and formations on the football field during halftime with the marching band. One weekend I choreographed group routines for every single song on the *Dazed and Confused* soundtrack. No one will know the struggles I had trying to develop a high-octane crowd pleaser to Foghat's "Slow Ride."

twins, as my mom likes to say, which is really just a nice way of saying, "Oops, we baked too much!" My sister and I could barely tolerate each other, so when one of us needed help, the other was all too happy to stand by holding a life preserver lit on fire. It's a typical dynamic among sisters: Be ruthless and competitive and nasty because you're fighting for a limited amount of attention and resources. At least that was the case between us. My parents won't be home for at least three hours. Audrey knows this, and she's enjoying her powerful position as gatekeeper. My friend Brooke is there, watching all of it. She has a brother and they love each other, so she doesn't get it, but she doesn't want to leave until I get inside. All I want is a shower. I spent two hours in the blazing Texas sun doing step ball changes to a dance remix of Toto's "Africa,"[3] a song about fifteen years past its prime[4] but was getting the resurgence it didn't deserve thanks to some asshole with DJ software. The heat, the sweat, my anger, Toto, it wells

---

3   We had to dance to hundreds of remixes that don't need to exist. I found videos of my high school drill team's recent competition dances and found two novelty dances—one to a dance remix of a song from *The Polar Express* (or "The Polor Express" as written on the mocked-up movie poster that served as their backdrop) and another to a dance remix of the *Smurfs'* theme. What's more humiliating than being a sixteen-year-old girl forced to wear white long-sleeved skintight spandex jumpsuits, painting your face and arms 1970s community-pool blue, then flawlessly incorporating jazz hands?

4   Honestly, who needs to snort coke in the bathroom of the Roxy listening to "I bless the rains down in Africa, gonna take some time to do the things we never had" at 128 bpm?

up inside me and I punch my hand through Audrey's window, which is surprisingly easy, not because I am strong, but because our house is flimsy. Blood is gushing out of my gangly wrist, so Brooke takes me to the emergency room, where they give me stitches. I still have two long scars on my right wrist that people think are suicide attempts until I explain, "These are the battle scars of sisterhood."[5]

My sister and I get along now, for the most part. We have cry-shout-finger-pointy fights every once in a while and then I have to check into a hotel and we don't speak for a day, but we always make up. We love each other now because we worked our shit out and we're not sharing a bathroom anymore. I hadn't thought about how much we used to beat the shit out of each other, and then last week I ate a pepper jelly that gave me some sort of allergic reaction and made me feel like I was burning alive from the inside out. It also brightened my scar tissue into glowing red secret messages from the past all over my arms and neck. All the evidence of our hatred showing up at once—scratches on my arms from nail fights,[6] burn marks from attacking each other with curling irons, bite marks. I thought, if I can survive all this at the hands of my sister, I can certainly take what-

---

5 People are more interested when they think they're suicide scars.

6 You have to have natural nails to cause damage. Tips don't do shit.

ever terrible shit awful powerful women are dishing out. Women who are making life (more) terrible for other women because they haven't gotten the memo about that behavior being retrograde as fuck. In their efforts to play a man's game to get to a position of power, they've aligned themselves against women. I don't think their minds can be changed, so we have to know who they are, be ready for their tactics, and just in case, have our 1½-inch metal barrel curling iron turned all the way hot.

Not all evil hags are easy to spot. Take Phyllis Schlafly. On paper, she's Rosie the Riveter fan fiction—worked as a ballistic gunner and technician at an ammunition plant during WWII, had a bunch of kids, THEN became a lawyer in the '70s, when about only 4 percent of lawyers were female. But in practice, she's what I call a Bizarro Gloria Steinem. It's as if upon Gloria's birth, the universe sought balance by creating an opposite, a ruthless sort of woman who would become successful in her male-dominated field, fighting gender stereotypes and breaking glass ceilings, then securing her throne by kicking other women off Progress Mountain before feasting on their carcasses. She was a constitutional lawyer, antifeminist, and all-around hate-filled human who makes Annie Wilkes look like Florence Nightingale. The good news is Phyllis Schlafly is dead. But before you tap-dance on her grave, we have to deal with the heinous stuff she did that is still not fixed. Like the Equal Rights Amendment (ERA)—which would have been a Constitutional guarantee of equal rights for women in the United States had she not stopped it from being passed. The ERA was ratified by thirty-five[7] states and was on track to get the thirty-eight states it needed to make the Constitution a cooler old dude. Like the kind of grandpa who used to be a staunch conservative but then started surfing and now he gives *you* weed. America was on the gender track to equality; then Phyllis Schlafly came riding through town on her hell horse STOP ERA, waving her villain's torch, warning the ERA[8] would take away the dignity and role of homemaker for women. Which makes no sense if you look at Phyllis's own mother, who single-handedly supported the family during the Great Depression while her father struggled with years of unemployment. My mom played her Tears for Fears record ad nauseum when I was a

---

7 It's since been ratified by two more—Nevada in 2017 and Illinois in 2018. Of the bottom-of-the-barrel states left, we only need one more. But which one is going to come through for us? Georgia? Florida? Arizona? Don't worry, Mississippi, you're off the hook. Nobody is counting on you to do the right thing…ever.

8 The deadline for ratifying the Equal Rights Amendment was March 22, 1979. On the day the most important piece of legislation for women's equality failed, I was born in Glendale, California. Fuck her for ruining the ERA and double fuck her for tarnishing the legacy of my birth.

kid, and even though I wanted to listen to "Stray Cat Strut," I didn't devote my adult life to legislating all copies of *Songs from the Big Chair* [9] be burned in a public fire.

TGPSID—Thank God Phyllis Schlafly Is Dead. But there are others like her. Women like Renee Ellmers, who became famous for a second when, as a representative of North Carolina in 2014, she begged Republican men to make their messaging to women clearer. She said:

> We need our male colleagues to understand that if you can bring it down to a woman's level and what everything that she is balancing in her life—that's the way to go.

"And what everything that she is balancing in her life." Cool sentence, bro. It's too easy to make fun of her for going all word crazy and using *what* with reckless abandon. It's too easy. I do elevated comedy. Like reading her for keeping scalloped necklines alive and kickin'. Renee, scallops are for old rich people without teeth to eat, not for decorating jacket lapels.

---

9 Plus, it wouldn't be the start of an exciting road trip if I couldn't play "Everybody Wants to Rule the World" as I'm pulling out of my driveway.

Her point is, "Hey, male politicians, talk to women like we're dumb because we're busy!" Or we're dumb and busy! We can't balance the triplets on our hips, marinate the chicken, put our hair in a French braid, do the dog's pedicure, AND concentrate on debt ceiling PowerPoint presentations filled with conservatively biased data! WE'VE GOT SHRINKY DINKS IN THE OVEN!

Renee objected to a provision in the "Pain-Capable Unborn Child Protection Act"—which is also my drag name—that would allow a woman seeking an abortion after twenty weeks' gestation to have the procedure if she was a victim of rape or incest. Renee said no, no, lady, you'll give birth to a criminal's baby and raise it and that's that! Not only is Renee putting trauma icing on top of an agony cake but also forcing the victim to be connected to the person who assaulted her forever. I've never been in this situation, but I can't imagine it's pleasant to drop your daughter off at your rapist's house for his custodial visits.

So, you see what kind of politically powerful, high-profile women to look out for, but what about Your Mom's Worst Friend, Deborah? You know this type of lady. All you want to do is relax from the plane, snuggle with Flea-ba McEntire, your mom's fourteen-year-old incontinent beagle, and drink wine out of a glass that holds an entire bottle of alcohol. BUT YOU CAN'T because Deborah's there.

She walks in without knocking, in her loud, colorful clothes and chunky necklaces[10] giving her the illusion of being a "laid-back fun-loving wine spritzer kind of gal." A go-with-the-flow kinda lady who doesn't mind if dinner plans change from fancy steak house to cheap hamburger joint; she's just there for the company! A woman just as comfortable in a Pier 1 as she is on an actual pier. But don't be fooled. She asked your mom for your flight information and hopped in her golf cart so she could be there the minute you arrive to get the scoop on how awful your life is since you ran away from Texas. Her thinly veiled questions—"How can you do improv at night *and* get a full night's rest for your job as a real estate receptionist?" and "Bars are open until 4:00 a.m.? Certainly you've just *heard* that, right, Erin? You're not *going* to those places?"—are small little judgments she's serving before she lays it all out on the table after dinner. "Erin, you have to get serious and find a nice smart man before no one wants you anymore." Then she looks at your mom and says, "Veronica, I've never had bread pudding this good!"

There are so many Your Mom's Worst Friend Deborahs out there. Suzanne Venker is my favorite example of this kind of peeking-over-the-hedges

---

10   Second reference for those chunky-necklace fans out there.

type of woman. I mentioned her briefly in the #MeToo chapter, but let's dig a little deeper. Suzanne is a politically correct–hating cultural critic and writer, out there bravely challenging the cultural norms with her endless supply of FoxNews.com essays. Brave essays like:

"I'm So Happy Trump's Not a 'Feminist.'"
"Are You Weak If You Make Your Man a Sandwich? This Is Why Real Men Don't Marry Feminists."
"Chivalry Is Dead Because Women Killed It."
"Most Men Just Want a Woman Who's Nice."
"It Isn't Men Who Are Toxic. It's Women."

Uh, I think there's a pattern here—Suzanne's lust for undermining women, probably from a safe little perch in her Colonial-style home, with her golden retriever sound asleep on a buffalo check bed, a fire roaring, and a hot cocoa screensaver on her TV screen, wrapped in a cashmere throw, filling the time she's not worrying about those Orvis winter socks arriving before hunting season. Your Mom's Worst Friend Deborah went to college to write the next *Cold Sassy Tree* but got sidetracked with her MS degree and ended up a kept woman mad at the loud women fighting for something greater than coordinating separates. Don't come to Your Mom's Worst

Friend Deborah whining about your clinical depression; she'll tell you to work harder. It'll make you wonder why your mom keeps inviting her over in the first place. Can they base a friendship on affinity for Robert Mondavi merlot alone?

They're bored rich moms with an outlet for their sad anger. Moms like Susan Patton, aka Princeton Mom, who in 2013 wrote an open letter to the *Daily Princetonian*, her alma mater's school newspaper, with advice for the "daughters she never had." Advice to pick a man PRONTO because they'll never be surrounded by such a quality stock of cock ever again. Susan argues in her letter that:

> As freshman women, you have four classes of men to choose from. Every year, you lose the men in the senior class, and you become older than the class of incoming freshman men. So, by the time you are a senior, you basically have only the men in your own class to choose from, and frankly, they now have four classes of women to choose from. Maybe you should have been a little nicer to these guys when you were freshmen?

Translated into an equation, it looks like this:

(4 classes of men/years in school) + the number of times you smiled = potential husbands.

Susan rode her wave of Internet virality and followed up with "A Little Valentine's Day Straight Talk" focusing on the postgrad working professional woman who is not spending enough time investing in finding a husband. It starts out with my favorite opening of any essay ever:

> Another Valentine's Day. Another night spent ordering in sushi for one and mooning over *Downton Abbey* reruns. Smarten up, ladies.

Joke's on Susan, she just perfectly described my ideal evening. You know what I did this Valentine's Day? Gave my dog a full-body massage and got wasted on hot toddies, then rewatched *Chef's Table* season 3 while my husband went to the Korean spa. And I'm happily married. Your Mom's Worst Friend Deborahs don't understand nuance at any level. They're grasping at the idea of traditional relationships because they're filled with bitterness, and it's not your responsibility to be the laundry basket for their misery towels and shame socks. Get a therapist, Deborah! And next time YMWFD tries to give you advice at your dad's luau-themed birthday party, put your hand on her shoulder and say, "I'm sorry your life is sad, Deborah," and then light a joint in front of her face and do not break eye contact.

At least with Bizarro Gloria Steinem or Your Mom's Worst Friend Deborah, they're pretty up front about what kind of people they are. But not That Lying Bitch. That Lying Bitch is all smiles and says all the right things to make you *think* she's on your side, like impassioned sentiments about women's health and pleas for sisterhood, but for real, she's an absolute sociopath. Which is fine when she's your friend's mimosa-addicted cousin from Cincinnati crashing brunch. Who cares? The only thing you lose is hours of your life listening to a thirty-three-year-old woman insisting she slept with Usher. But when she's in the White House, there's a lot more at stake.

Ivanka Trump,[11] as you may or may not know, is the special assistant to the U.S. president, a title no one has ever had because it's as made-up as any statistic her father has ever referenced. I guess her job is to trick her father into not doing the worst things while also allegedly working on female-bolstering initiatives, but so far she's accomplished nothing, which might be too harsh to say. Let me rephrase that: She's done everything she can with the shallow well of courage she was born with.

Ivanka is a complicated person who grew up in

---

11   Ivanka has the wettest teeth of anyone I've ever seen. Her lips move around on them like two children on a Slip'N Slide.

a world none of us could imagine. In her book *The Trump Card: Playing to Win in Work and Life*, she writes about how her dad arranged to have Michael Jackson watch her dance in a school production of the *Nutcracker*. *My* dad used to hang from our apricot tree and say, "Me monkey man—me shake fruit," and my sister and I would scurry across the ground like rats, using our mouths to pick up the fruit he shook off the tree. Ivanka operates on a different plane of existence than the rest of us rodent cosplayers. Her money and pseudo status allow her to be a hypocrite. She can talk about the importance of American jobs while manufacturing her clothes overseas. She can express sympathy for the terrorism victims in Barcelona but ignore domestic terrorists in Charlottesville. She can talk about reproductive care while her dad rolls back birth control coverage.[12]

Ivanka expresses the importance of paid maternity leave while giving none to her own employees. She rallies to close the gender pay gap, then publicly supports her father as he ends Obama's initiatives to eradicate said gap. She talks about how damaging sexual assault is while ignoring the fact her father likely raped her mother and attacked any number

---

12   I just want to reiterate, and I know you all already know it, but for the three straight guys reading this book, I want to stress, birth control is necessary because I am tired of cum in my belly button. Everyone wants it on the inside!

of women, including a thirteen-year-old girl who filed a civil suit claiming she was attacked by Donald Trump at an orgy in the home of registered sex offender Jeffrey Epstein. But blaming Ivanka's wealth for her lack of follow-through is too easy. She hasn't done shit because Ivanka Trump is a conniving soulless scag.

If my dad publicly called me "a piece of ass" or told *The View* if I weren't his daughter he'd be dating me, I would have taken my MILLIONS of dollars out of my personal bank account and dedicated my life to destroying my father. One time I was at dinner with my dad and the waitress said, "And what will your girlfriend be having to drink?" and he was about to order for me and I was like, "Nonononononononononooo, I'm not doing this Woody Allen Roman Polanski bullshit one-act play with you tonight."

But it doesn't even affect her. It can't affect her. She's a perfect Trump Jr. (sorry not sorry, actual Trump Jr.): emotionless, ruthless, and willing to lie to protect her shitty empire. An empire built on footwear suspiciously similar to Italian shoe designs and books filled with other people's TED Talks. What person does all that and then is willing to be a scapegoat for her father's bad behavior? She just stands there while he says things like, "How could I be sexist? I made her," or "How can I hate the Jews? She fucks one." She feels nothing. She is the Terminator. And for bucking gender norms, "you go, girl" I guess?

Sure, Ivanka's a liar and a schemer and an opportunist, but the worst thing about her is she's fucking BORING! On her Instagram she writes about the things she claims to be passionate about with the verve of a sloth coming out of a coma. She repeats the same sentence over and over again on her Instagram account:

- It was an honor to attend the FIRST Robotics Competition
- Honored to lead the United States delegation to this year's Global Entrepreneurship Summit
- It was an honor to meet the Medal of Valor recipients.

You know what people who truly care do? Use different words. I'm passionate about my dislike of Ivanka Trump. And it's a real passion, so I can come up with names for her like Flesh Stiletto; What an American Express Platinum Card Would Sound and Look Like If a Wizard Brought It to Life; 'Lil Eva Braun; Marzipan Gams; Walking Blood Diamond; Aryan Crayola; Complicity Huffman; Shiksa von Swastika. And I can come up with all those different words because they're not manufactured sentiment.

So when you see her fake-ass social media presence and her counterfeit compassion, remember she means none of it. She probably doesn't even write it. I bet she pays a dead-eyed sixteen-year-old Deerfield boarding student to run her Instagram in exchange for a carton of Dunhills. The point is, Ivanka might look like a Barney's mannequin with the vocabulary of a ten-year-old nerd, but here's who she really is—she's the ice queen who tells you you're not good enough to be in the first row at SoulCycle. Who after class looks at you and says, "Maybe you should stick to Zumba." That's who she really is.

But let her keep lying. Let Suzanne Venker write her garbage; let Phyllis Schlafly's ghost float around Stone Mountain.[13] We don't need them to change the way they are. We need better women to replace them.

Since the election of Donald Trump, an avalanche of women have kick-started their political careers. According to EMILY's List, as of spring 2018, over twenty-one thousand women have signed up to run for office. That's half a Lilith Fair!

It's exciting! But we need all of you to run and be bold! Dana Nessel—who is running for Michigan State's attorney general office—made an amazing ad posing the very serious question, "Who can you trust

---

13 The confederate Mt. Rushmore; carved sloppily into the side of a giant rock are the faces of Robert E. Lee, Stonewall Jackson, and Jefferson Davis. It's a great Saturday trip from Atlanta if you're looking to punch a Nazi.

to not show you their penis in a professional setting? The candidate without one." And if you're not gonna run, you need to get out there and support the women who are! Let's show the world how great women run shit!

PERIODS DON'T JUST RUIN PANTIES, THEY RUIN FREEDOM

Here's a biology lesson for the uninitiated: Women between the ages of Shiloh Jolie-Pitt and Julianne Moore bleed out of their bottom hole once a month. These blood tears are cried by our no-baby uteruses as a sign to us and to others that, for at least another month, we're still eating for one. Periods might sound like a time to celebrate the glorious powers of a woman's nature, which if you believe that, good news, you're actually a mythical wood elf! Or a hippie mom dressed head to toe in String Cheese Incident crinkle skirt regalia who throws moon ceremony parties for your embarrassed daughters. In either case, you are free to traipse across the forest floor and make your own fudge cookies and look stupid in green button-down vests. For the REAL people reading this, be warned. This chapter is full of brutal truths about periods, how much they cost, how much they hurt, the shame, and how little anyone cares. Grab a stiff drink, and then grab another, and then a third. Have a fourth ready just in case. Wheel your CB2 drink cart over to your couch or bed, wherever you're reading this. Have a puke bucket ready and the phone number for poison control.

Okay, now you're ready to read on.

Periods can suck a big donkey cock. They can wrap their metaphorical lips around the veiny eighteen-inch, sun-wrinkled dong of a work horse and go to town. It's all they deserve. For child-free women, like me, who would like to remain without babies, the only upside to my period is the sweet relief when it's finally over. I would rip out my own uterus but then I'd have to deal with menopause, which is the sequel no one asked for.[1] I hate my period so much I pretend it doesn't exist. Which means, once a month, I am randomly attacked by my own body with NO warning.[2] The ONLY good thing my period has done for me is provide me with a lifetime prescription to Tramadol, which curbs my body-crippling cramps and helps me get through small talk at lame Hollywood dinner parties. I can't begin to describe how much easier it is to get

---

1   Periods are *Grownups*, and menopause is *Grownups II*.
2   Lots of predictable warnings.

through being talked at by a guy[3] who can't shut up about his Eric Roberts horse friendship movie when I'm high on pain pills. I'm actually suddenly interested in what this stranger[4] is droning on about. "Oh, you should cast Paula Patton as the love interest. Maybe put a racetrack explosion in Act II!"

I found Tramadol when I went to my doctor and described my symptoms and he knew just what I needed and wrote a prescription. Just kidding! Doctors don't understand period pain. It was a Saturday and I was crumpled up like a dirty, soaking-wet towel on my bed, begging God to have some mercy and let me die. Then I remembered something important. I called my ex-husband, who had just recovered from spine surgery. Back surgery is no joke, and neither were the meds they gave him. Over the phone, I whispered something about "help" and "pills" and he came over as fast as he could. Michael laid them all out on my doorstep, like a blackjack dealer, and ran away. He'd been married to me; he knew what was happening inside—a feral cat woman crawling out of bed and walking on all fours to the front door. And I do mean crawl. My cramps are so intense, it hurts to stand up or straighten my body. John Guillebaud, a professor of reproductive health

---

3   It was Steven Spielberg.
4   It was not Steven Spielberg.

at University College London,[5] said periods can feel "almost as bad as having a heart attack"—which is why I was dragging myself, hands and knees, to my front door, where five beautiful 300 mg Tramadol waited patiently for me in a ziplock bag. In forty minutes, I was a functional human being, thanks to someone else's synthetic narcotics.

Armed with my new street knowledge, I asked my primary care doctor for Tramadol. I told him I have terrible cramps and this is what works and he wrote me a prescription, which he continues to write every year, without offering another solution 'cause he doesn't have one. And not one gynecologist has ever asked me about my menstrual pain management. No one asks because they don't have the answers. Scientists and pharmaceutical companies aren't doing research on period pain, so doctors don't know how to treat it. NorthShore University director of gynecological pain Frank Tu told Quartz some physicians are taught that ibuprofen "should be good enough." Ibuprofen isn't strong enough to treat anything. Taking Ibuprofen for my period cramps is like throwing a cup of water on the sun.

Richard Legro at Penn State College of Medicine found evidence that Viagra could treat cramp pain

5   Pick an educational descriptor. Is it a "university" or a "college"? Do they offer course classes there to become an attorney lawyer?

but no one will fund more research. He said, "I've applied three or four times but it always gets rejected. I think the bottom line is nobody thinks menstrual cramps is an important public health issue."

Well, half the population thinks it's an issue, but there's this problem we have where doctors take our pain less seriously.[6] So who will listen?

I felt a glimmer of hope about a tiny pain-fighting device you can wear on your belt. It's called Livia, and it uses small adhesive pads placed on your belly to stimulate your nerves and somehow block the pain from reaching your brain. It sounds kind of like electroshock therapy for your ovaries, but it beats my old method of hooking jumper cables to my labia and revving the engine. Livia can be yours for $149, but, as San Fran ob-gyn Jen Gunter points out on her blog, she's been prescribing them for years, under their non-sexy name, TENS units, which you can get right now online for $35. They're not as flashy or cool as the Livia—Livia looks like fun lady stickers and the TENS unit looks like something ghost hunters use to detect energy vortexes—but it's certainly a cheaper investment. I bought a TENS unit. Does it work? Um, maybe? I am so afraid of not taking my new pain medicine—Duexis—I can't conduct a

---

6   If you want to get super angry, read Joe Fassler's *Atlantic* piece "How Doctors Take Women's Pain Less Seriously."

thorough experiment. But if it doesn't work, I only lost $35! I do use it on my sore muscles after I work out. Does it work? WHO KNOWS! It definitely does *something.* If someone can come up with a foolproof cure for menstrual pain, they could charge whatever they want and we'll buy it. They'll be so rich, Saudi princes will look like Little Orphan Annie.

The legalization of weed is attracting all kinds of medicinal research, and a lot of companies are focusing on menstrual relief. Cannabis companies are investing heavily in products for pain relief, but I am less than enthused by this future. Last time I went to my weed store, I had to talk to a blitzed dude about what they had for period pain. He told me about THC + CBD vaginal suppositories. Well, I bought them, and I used them, and then I found out a year later they're not approved for internal use. What is the THC and CBD suspended in? I don't know 'cause it's not listed on the company's website. What did I shove up my pussy? Coconut oil? Petroleum? Crisco? Is it shocking that a company cashing in on the menstrual pain market run by two dudes assumed we were so desperate for pain relief we'd shove anything up there? Anyway, it's been up there for two years and still occasionally emits a high-pitched beep. I'm sure it's fine, although it's weird that the sound summons birds.

While I am prepared to spend however much it

takes at the weed store to manage my shark week, women shouldn't be forced to rely on a dispensary for help navigating their menstrual pain. Pot shop employees should know the differences between indicas and sativas; they shouldn't be forced to become our period pain shamans. Being counseled about my crimson waves by a dude in a *Rick and Morty* T-shirt just seems like a phenomenal misuse of human resources. He should be free to do what he does best—sharing socialist memes on Reddit or whatever—and I should have a fucking period pain cure by now.

We're groping in the dark for a period fix that should already be FDA approved—and women are spending far too much money looking for relief.

It's not just period pain that's expensive—so are the tampons and pads we shove up our meaty paper towel tubes.

If dudes had periods, tampons would be free in public restrooms (like toilet paper already is). Tampons would be displayed in brandy snifters or in a hollowed-out football signed by [FOOTBALL HERO WHO NEVER ABUSED DOGS OR WOMEN]. These manpons wouldn't be housed in a janky 1982 vending machine covered in rust that only takes PHYSICAL quarters and men would never have to shove a Reagan-era, rock-hard column of petrified cotton up their manginas as their only recourse to stop the bleeding from ruining their boxer briefs.

Those manpons certainly wouldn't be taxed like tampons. Absorb this![7]—tampons are subject to sales tax in thirty-eight states because they are not classified as medical necessities. Name something you BLEED into that's not a medical necessity. And don't say "Edward Cullen's mouth." It doesn't count.

The "medical necessity" label is an arbitrary classification made by, I dunno, a tax code drunk who is bad at his job but can't be fired because he's got dirt on a higher-up? It's the only explanation I can think of for why some dandruff shampoos, lip balms, and condoms are classified as medical necessities and are therefore tax exempt. A horny, flaky-scalped, lizard-lipped man gets a free tax ride but I have to pay an extra 9 percent to soak up my monthly Nightmare on Panty Street? Even some cotton balls are tax exempt! Ques que le difference, tax code? A tampon is just an orgy of cotton balls climbing a gym-class rope up into my crampy vagina. Tampons are subject to sales tax because they are considered a *luxury item*. You know, private jets, infinity pools, superabsorbency tampons. I can't think of anything more luxurious than shoving a glorified sponge to stop my gushing lower mezzanine.

It's not hard to eliminate the tampon tax. It's so

---

7   Official name of my ska band. I will sue if you try and use this!

easy Canada did it, and they need the money! What kind of industries do they even have? Carly Rae Jepsen? Terrible pizza? Apologies? Canada got rid of their tampon tax in 2015, but in the United States, progress on this issue is a slow drip down the leg of justice. Twelve states don't tax tampons, but five of them don't have any sales tax anyway. Now you're left with seven states, with Illinois and New York the latest to jump on the toll-free, jumbo tampon expressway. But take California, where I currently bleed. Tampon tax revenue is so substantial, when Governor Jerry Brown had the chance to eliminate the tax in 2016, he said the state couldn't afford to lose it. I can think of much better ways to contribute to California's bottom line:

- Tickets for people who get in fights in the West Hollywood Whole Foods parking lot. Last week I saw two men screaming at each other, one of them holding a half gallon of juiced wheatgrass. The fight looked like it was over something important but was probably over whether or not coconut oil pulling actually fights gingivitis. They should make these yoga clowns have to pay for the public disturbance.
- Fines for every tourist who stops me at the Grove and asks, "Where do the Kardashians shop?" Right now I'm teaching them a lesson and send-

ing them to American Girl Place, which I consider to be the most frightening spot in Los Angeles. While these unsuspecting tourists slowly realize they don't want to be in there, they'll spend a frantic half hour trying to find the exit, surrounded by hundreds of dolls, leering intensely with their overly dilated painted-on pupils. Stare at them long enough and a shiver will run down your spine. Stay too long and fall prey to their bloodthirst.

- Jail time for people at parties who talk about whether or not they're eating bread right now.

Not only would this new tax revenue line California's pockets, but it would also make my day-to-day life 80 percent more palatable.

There's no way to track what California does with the roughly $20 million they make annually in tampon taxes. I'm not sure I want to know. I already hate so many things about California—the lack of resources for the homeless, the chronic fires, the cost of living, Russell Brand showing up essentially naked to my hot yoga class—I don't need another thing on the list. Women in the UK found out £250,000 of their tampon taxes were going to Life, an anti-choice group that, along with sixty-nine other women's organizations, won a bid for funding. Women protested and gathered signatures to have the money revoked, but the government assured everyone that Life promised to use the money to help women in need and not to spread their anti-choice platform. Um, okay, I don't believe them. What are they going to do, lead low-income women inside while instructing them to pay no attention to the posters of a crying Jesus floating over fetal tissue? If Life wants to keep tampon tax money flowing in, they better get on board the pro-choice wagon or they're gonna be out of business with all those non-menstruating pregnant women running around.

The money state governments make is microscopic compared to what the tampon companies are bringing in. Tampax, Kotex, and Playtex are all getting large cuts of the $15 billion tampon industry, without specifically talking about or showing what their products do. Kotex ran a "revolutionary" campaign making fun of tampon commercial tropes, tampons soaking up blue liquids and periods preventing us from doing what we love most—frolicking in lavender fields and flying kites. But in their efforts to make fun of the ways commercials dance around this biological function, they, too, avoided using the words *vagina* or *blood*—two main components of Operation: Menstruation. If I have to be subjected to a Lamisil commercial where a purple and yellow animated toe fungus, with the voice of a New Jersey cigar dad, props open a toenail like a car hood and crawls inside like a worm, tampon companies should be able to run commercials like this:

INT. BATHROOM—MIDNIGHT

A sleepy woman shuffles into the bathroom. She pulls down her leggings and plops her unshaven thighs on the toilet and shuts the door. The dog scratches frantically on the other side. The woman thrusts a wad of toilet paper between her legs, then pulls it up to reveal gobs of body marinara. She sighs, then leans down to reach under the sink. She opens the cabinet door, leaving a bloody fingerprint on the corner. She uses her blood-free hand to pull out a humidifier, nail polish remover, Epsom salt, and a crusty vibrator she's been looking for. Then she finds it—a half-open tampon, barely clean. She blows hair and dust off and shoves it into her tired vagina. She wipes her hands on the red floor mat, leaving no visible evidence. She flushes the toilet and opens the door. Off to the kitchen to find leftover muscle relaxers. The dog rushes in and licks the bloody fingerprint.

FADE TO BLACK.

In 2013, Tampax released a new line of tampons—Tampax Radiant. They don't glow in the dark or come packed with a nuclear core reactor. They do something much more impressive. According to their website,[8] Tampax Radiant tampons are "protection you can keep secret" because of the "redesigned discreet wrapper that is softer and quieter." Oh, a quiet wrapper! Perfect for all those times I've needed to publicly change my tampon during *Hamilton*.

All of this is a form of control, to keep us entangled in period problems, and it's not just the U.S. government doing this; period shame is built into religions that view menstrual cycles as spiritually dangerous and the women having them as unclean, keeping girls from going to school, and banishing them to a period tent for days regardless of the weather. In 2017, Nepal tried to outlaw the Hindu menstrual tradition chhaupadi after a woman, who was banished to a cow shed during her period, was bitten by a snake and died. The same year, a twelve-year-old girl in India killed herself after she was shamed for a period stain by her teacher. This is real and a disgusting way to treat a biological function responsible for life. How about instead of sending

---

8   If you want to see something unimaginable, go to Tampax's website and watch their video on insertion in which two teens penetrate a child's pool floatie with a tampon.

women to raggedy tents during an intense bodily transformation, we celebrate this beautiful, life-giving moment and send women to a menstrual spa, where they can wrap themselves in down-filled blankets and watch as many episodes of *90 Day Fiancé* as they want? Want a macaroni and grilled cheese sandwich for breakfast? No problem. Want to look at a Crate & Barrel catalog and cry? Go to town! Want to cut your bangs? No, lady, think about it.

There are women here to help. Jennifer Weiss-Wolf's book *Periods Gone Public* is a great resource if you want to learn everything you ever wanted to know about your body. If you're in a major city or a smaller city with a large population of socialists driving Volvos running on vegetable oil, you can get one-on-one or group counseling with a period coach. They're sort of like a baseball coach, except they're only concerned with home plate. Erica Chidi Cohen, of LOOM in Los Angeles, sat me in a comfy chair, led me through a light meditation, then calmly explained all the functions of my menstrual cycle to me. The whole session was very emotional. First, I felt so dumb for not knowing this stuff. Then I was angry a gynecologist had never discussed any of this with me.[9]

---

9   According to my friends who have taken fertility meds, they got a brief lesson on how their menstrual cycle works and the hormones involved from their doctors because it's important to time their shots right. So, lessons on the menstrual cycles from doctors are reserved

By the end, I was just happy someone took the time to help me understand my own body. She got me to track my period with the free app Clue so I know what is happening with my hormones now and how they're affecting my brain and my body. All vacations are now planned around my period. If you see me anywhere else but L.A., you can bet I'm not bleedin'. The other cool thing about the app is you can share your cycle with anyone who won't use the information against you. "Oh babe, you're premenstrual! No wonder you're pissed I left my wet towel on your work clothes!" Erica also showed me how to use a menstrual cup (I use Saalt), which I was so afraid of before because I could not conceptualize how I shoved a little plastic orange-juice-cup-looking thing into my vagina, but now I'm jamming it up there like a pro. Plus, I'm taking my money away from tampon manufacturers, which makes me giddy.

Periods are punk as fuck and our bodies are fucking magic. I refuse to stand by while people villainize my miraculous blood time or charge me extra for it. When I go to Starbucks, I tell them my name is "menstruation" and then I proudly pick up my venti iced tea with extra water and light ice and

---

only for when you're using your period to make a baby, not to understand why, on the sixteenth day of your cycle, you cry in your car.

saunter out like I fucking own the world. When I'm hiking up Runyon Canyon with cramps and I see some lazy man whining up the hill, I kick him in the shins and scream, "If I can bleed up this hill, you can walk up it—weenis!" C'mon, everybody! Feel your menstrual joy! Let's make period stigma like dial-up modems and Will Smith seeming happy: ancient fucking history.

BANKRUPTING THE MAKEUP MEN

When I tell you I grew up poor, I don't mean it in the way most white people say it—like they had to share a bathroom with an older brother and their first car was their bank manager mom's ten-year-old Nissan Maxima.

My family was "selling homegrown green beans off of I-40 on a Saturday" poor. "Spanked for draining perfectly hot bath water" poor. "Merry Christmas! Your present is continued health" poor. "Certified pre-owned wardrobe" poor. But, somehow, my mom found extra cash to buy herself Lancôme makeup. In the early '80s, the makeup line wasn't the "dollar bin" brand it is now. Wearing Lancôme meant you were rich and knew a French word other than Jean Naté. Every year, my mom would buy three expensive Lancôme items: foundation, eye shadow, and lipstick, which, in our below-the-poverty-line world, doubled as blush. She would put on her face, like a glamazon, and go to work at the pet store, where she fed live baby bunnies to snakes. And I think it's beautiful that the last thing those sweet little fur balls saw was my mom's perfectly applied $40 eye shadow.

I grew up thinking makeup made women better, more beautiful, worthy of love. It allowed us to transcend our station in life. I might have just eaten a $5 Trader Joe's lentil wrap in a gas station parking lot, but my brow filler says I had $45 crab claws and a glass of lightly effervescent rosé at Chateau Marmont.

And while I totally accept that makeup is a tool of oppression wielded by the patriarchy to make us conform to "normal" beauty standards, I also think makeup is fun! I love the way I look when I have it on. I love filling in my eyebrows, changing the shape of my eyes, putting subtle glitter on my cheeks. The Buddhist monks have their sand art; I have satin jewel tone eye shadow palettes. Spending hours getting the blending right only to wash it off in the shower five hours later is an exercise of the transitory nature of material life. Makeup is a personal choice and I would never judge another woman for the amount of cosmetics she puts on her face. What I do have a problem with is who is getting rich off our beauty bucks.

One day, high on sativa lemonade, I was slowly

applying my NARS Train Bleu lip pencil—a dark, almost black lipstick that makes people not talk to me at the airport. I was having all sorts of deep thoughts about who would invent such a bold color and then what genius had the idea to put it in a pencil! Then, I wondered, who owns NARS?

Turns out: men. And they own almost all the other major cosmetics companies too.

This wasn't always the case. In the beginning, the beauty market was a closed circle. Women paid women for their cosmetics. Beauty industry titans like Helena Rubinstein and Elizabeth Arden were swimming in cash before it was legal for them to vote. By convincing the women of the day to look and smell like a fancy harlot, they kick-started a new brand of mini-empires that grew into the completely recession-proof, $95 BILLION industry it is today. These female queens of cosmetics made tons of money, but instead of building brands their daughters could run, sold their companies, went public, or died without a will ensuring the business fell into the soft, well-manicured hands of a woman.

I should have known the industry was run by men. The signs were there all along. I worked at the Estée Lauder counter[1] at Macy's Willowbrook Mall

---

1   I wanted to work at the Chanel counter but the woman who ran it was a sour bitch who didn't like me.

during college, so off I went to the required one-day training session taught by Estée professionals, involving eight full hours of learning fake scientific phrases like "concentrate matrix" and "synchronized recovery." We got a free, delicious lunch consisting of a soggy ham sandwich and off-brand BBQ potato chips. At the end of the day, they handed us plastic bags with our official Estée Lauder uniform—a navy polyester dress with matching lab coat. Polyester layered on polyester is a body-suffocating combo, and the shape made me look less like a makeup artist and more like a joyless Universalist wedding officiant. The uniform was not built to accommodate bending over, which was a large part of my job. All the products were stocked below the counter and to get them, I had to make a dramatic move, like how screen actresses would faint in the '40s, collected but distressed. I would sit on the floor, side saddle, grab the product, then hop into a squat, rising slowly, keeping my back arched, tilting my pelvis forward so my uniform wouldn't expose my panties to the general public. I did that yoga routine for two years. Any woman in a position of power would see how absolutely insane the uniform was and would have ordered them all thrown into a pile, doused in gasoline, then lit on fire while we all watched them melt into a gooey navy Youth Dew–scented plastic bonfire. But that never happened on account of all the golf cocks dominating the C-suite at Estée Lauder.

On their website, Estée Lauder brags about 51 percent of their senior VP and above positions being held by women. Not impressive. It's the corporate equivalent of getting a D on a test and bragging that it's not an F. In a fair and just world, their corporate org chart would be littered with vaginas (except for Terrence, their sole male executive, who knows how to contour like a motherfucker and out–smoky eye a raccoon).

Estée Lauder CEO Fabrizio Freda is one of the highest paid CEOs in America, and the only CEO with the name of an Italian odor eliminator. "Guiseppe's dirty football socks are no match for Fabrizio! Grazie, Mama!" He's making a cool $48.4 million a year. It's a hard number to conceptualize,[2] so let's break it down in smaller terms. He makes $132,602 A DAY!!!! He makes $5,525 AN HOUR! $92 A MINUTE!! "I worked three minutes today, sushi dinner is on me!" Fabrizio is so rich he can afford to melt gold coins and throw them into hurricanes.

One of the reasons Fabrizio is so stupid rich is because he's turned Estée Lauder into a writhing,

---

2   Like when someone on the History Channel tries to convey the size of an ancient Incan city by explaining how many football fields could fit inside. I don't understand what that means! Can't we just say it was the size of Cincinnati?

stinking cosmetic rat king, tangling its tail with Aveda, Bobbi Brown, Bumble and bumble, Clinique, Jo Malone, La Mer, MAC, Origins, Smashbox, Too Faced, and the company getting most of my money: Le Labo. Le Labo fragrances make me smell like an elderly rich Milanese woman who refuses to use a walker no matter the costs. I'll break a hip tryin' to get up a curb, but I'll fill that ambulance with the smell of sandalwood and cedar. Le Labo has this special line inspired by the greatest cities in the world (not you, Kansas City, you stanky pile of BBQ detritus) that is only available for the month of September. Why September? Probably because some number dork at corporate turned in a report showing low sales in September and then Ethan, their self-proclaimed "marketing genius" who just graduated from Harvard Business School, said, "This might sound crazy, but I was at 1 OAK last night mainlining 1982 Château Angelus and getting crunk off of Kumamotos when it hit me—I think people will buy more stuff if we make it impossible to get." And then they clapped so hard they gave themselves hard-ons. Would a WOMAN-OWNED business do this? No. Women know our hard days are unpredictable. What if we get laid off suddenly in April and then in May we find out our boyfriend has a secret girlfriend in Toronto? Maybe by June we need to buy a fucking perfume to have something beautiful in our life for a change. A woman-owned business wouldn't say to us, "Sorry, you'll just have to wait until late fall." Why does male-run Estée Lauder–owned Le Labo want to keep us from moving on with our lives?!

In the male-dominated cosmetics world, there's no company quite like Revlon. Their ex-CEO Lorenzo Delpani is, in my opinion, the devil's cum stain, and a whole garbage truck of ColorStay foundation wouldn't be able to cover up his wrongdoings. First of all, he's more than happy to fund his lavish, open-shirted Bugatti lifestyle with sales from Revlon's eye shadow, a terrible product that only shows up on lid skin after four thousand applications. The only way I like to see Revlon cosmetics is flattened by an electric wheelchair on the floor at CVS. Their products belong in the city dump, if that's even a thing we have anymore. We might be dumping things directly into the Pacific Ocean these days.

Secondly, according to a discrimination lawsuit brought by Revlon's top scientist, Alan Meyers,[3] Delpani is one of those no-holds-barred assholes who finds unique ways to be awful to everyone. Like ignoring factory safety concerns, forcing Alan to act like a human easel during business meetings, expressing genuine confusion as to why there weren't

---

3   You'd think cosmetic companies would have women click-clacking their heels all up and down their scientific divisions. Nope.

more Jewish people at Revlon because "Jews" stick together, which is just slightly less terrible than the allegation that Delpani claimed he could smell black people when they walked in the room. Yes, you read that horrific sentence correctly—he said he can smell black people. If Meyers is telling the truth, Delpani might not be the world's biggest racist, but he is definitely the most inventive. Who knew a projections expert and outstanding public speaker also has an innovative outlook on racial intolerance?

When this all came out in the press, the company denied everything and "amicably" settled with Myers. Delpani continued on as CEO for another couple of years until he "stepped down" for "personal reasons." And by "stepped down" they mean "he's still on the board and is being paid as an adviser."

At least Revlon has a 33 percent female board;[4] Coty, on the other hand, had ZERO women in their senior management until 2017 (they now have one). I know, I know. "Who the fuck is Coty?" you ask. Turns out they're a massive umbrella company, and according to their website, not only are they dominating the fragrance game, but they're also number two for salon color and number three in color cosmetics. They own a ton of wildly successful

---

4   According to CNN Money.

brands—Calvin Klein fragrance, CoverGirl, Marc Jacobs fragrance, Philosophy, O.P.I., Rimmel, Clairol, Wella, Sebastian, Nioxin, and Sally Hansen. It is truly sad there's not a gaggle of women lording over Sally Hansen, because she might be my favorite cosmetics heroine. The woman DESERVES a movie, a good one, where she's played by Cate Blanchett doing her best "I'm indifferent to how much I hate loving you" acting. Outside of being a very successful businesswoman at a time when that sort of success would get a bitch burned at the stake, Sally Hansen had three husbands and zero children. The '40s must have been a great time to be a divorced woman without kids; I bet people were super cool about it.

Hansen was a regular beauty columnist for the *LA Times*, where she once penned the iconic line, "Personal charm often is more desirable than startling physical beauty." She was preaching the truth while selling lies! She was yin and yang. Fire and water. Dwight Yoakam and Method Man. Oh, and if this amazing list isn't enough for you, one of her best friends was trans. In the '40s!!!!!!! If you gave me a time machine, I would not go back to kill baby Hitler; I would go back and be friends with Sally Hansen.

Today, Trans-Friend No-Children's beautiful legacy is being run by men. What if women, and women exclusively, were getting rich off button-downs with anime characters on them, Bud Light mirrors, *Deadpool* masks, Packers season tickets, and everything else the worst guy from college is spending his stupid money on? Huh, think about that and maybe then you can understand my outrage, one straight guy reading this book because your school is making you do so as punishment.

It's not surprising that these traditional, prehistoric companies have such retrograde practices, but if you're thinking newer, emerging companies are any better, you're in for some depressing news.

You might know Rihanna's Fenty line, a cosmetics line so inclusive it makes Benetton look like the KKK. They have over forty different foundation shades and a yellow highlighter that I would punch a toddler in the face for. While it's true Rihanna[5] is the face and founder and blah blah blah of the company, the line was created by Kendo. Kendo is run by David Suliteanu, who used to be the CEO of Sephora. Kendo is run by a man and owned by another male-run luxury beauty company, LVMH aka Louis Vuitton Moët Hennessy—the world's largest luxury brand umbrella company. Louis Vuitton and Moët joining forces is the luxury brand equivalent of air and water merging.

---

5   I'm not saying you shouldn't buy Fenty. I'm just saying you should know all the players involved.

LVMH is run by Bernard Arnault, the fourth-richest person in the world and the richest person in France. Full disclosure, I don't like most French people. They're mean as a rule and when I see a French person smile, I get scared because they're about to do something fucked up. Every minute in Paris that I wasn't eating was a nightmare. I asked a saleswoman at Le Bon Marché, IN FRENCH, if I could try on some shoes and she just said, "NO" then walked away. I don't like the French and I don't like a French man sitting on $85.8 billion he made off the hard-earned dollars of (underpaid) women. What's he gonna spend it on, anyway? Stuffed goose livers and imperiousness?

With essentially every major cosmetics brand lining the pockets of some dude, we are then left with one woman—Kylie Jenner. From my research, it looks like Kylie's Lip Kit empire is run by women, or by just her and her mom. But who knows how long it'll last. Kris Jenner recently told *Women's Wear Daily*:

If one of the big ones came along and was to buy Kylie, I think it would be a very exciting time, but also a time for great growth and it would give Kylie a whole new world to create in.

Here's a sentence I thought I'd never write—PLEASE, KYLIE, DON'T SELL YOUR COS-

METICS BUSINESS! WOMEN NEED YOU! The cosmetics industry is hard enough to break into and you did it, sister! You should also be proud to be the first Kardashian/Jenner to create a valuable product not shot on a camcorder!

There's a great Mr. Rogers saying I would like to use inappropriately to transition to my next section of thoughts. He said, "When I was a boy and I would see scary things in the news, my mother would say to me, 'Look for the helpers. You will always find people who are helping.'" So, let's look for the helpers. And buy their eyeliner.

Go into your Clinique bag stained with bronzer, because it's time to fill it with these wonderful 100 percent female-owned, conscientious cosmetic lines.

SKIN CARE

My Lancôme Crème Radiance now lives in my garbage can, alongside onion shavings and a DVD of *Cats*. Not only did Lancôme founder Armand Petitjean use horse blood in his early moisturizers, Lancôme fired sexy weirdo Isabella Rossellini at forty-two to hire a younger spokeswoman. Then, in 2016, they hired her back at sixty-three. She told the *Cut* that a person showed up on a motorcycle, took off their helmet, and long blond hair fell out. Isabella asked, "What happened?" and the female exec responded, "Things change." And then rode off into the sunset. Now, I don't know if the scenario as described is what really happened or if a board meeting retelling got put through the Rossellini storytelling machine, but I hope more than anything it's true because that's the exact life I picture Isabella Rossellini having.

Thank God for my friend Jennie Pierson, who told me about oil cleansing. After a hard day in Los Angeles of driving one mile in three hours, I only have the energy to slop one thing on my face, and it better do everything, so I've been using Marie Veronique's Replenishing Oil Cleanser. I barely use half a pump and my face is clean and not left stripped.[6] You have to shake it every time to mix up the product, but all that means is it's natural. Ever seen Hidden Valley Italian dressing next to homemade Italian dressing? HVI never separates because it's bonded by nuclear corporate waste. Marie Veronique isn't just an esthetician; she's got both a math and a science degree and was trained to succeed in the ruthless beauty industry by teaching high school chemistry. I know teenagers are now the saviors of America and will

---

6   Also, do yourself a favor and buy ten black washcloths. They're
     hella cheap and let you wipe off as much mascara as you want and
     you don't have to ruin your good washcloths.

destroy the NRA, but when I was in high school, we used to make fun of our chemistry teacher for raising rabbits, so I gotta believe there are still a lot of shitty teens out there. Oh, and when Marie Veronique doesn't want to tinker in her face lab alone, she calls up her daughter, who is a physicist and biomedical engineer, to collaborate. Who would you rather give money to—a millionaire man who makes his money by torturing rabbits with unnecessary makeovers or two earth witches harnessing the power of science to gently squeeze skin-healing properties out of a delicate rose petal?

TONER/MOISTURIZER

If you work out to curb your anxiety so you don't chew all the skin off your lips like me, pop Thayers Rosewater Tonic Wipes, run by CEO Karen Clarke, in your gym bag to wipe away all your nasty acne-causing sweat. And if it's super dry outside, because we're living in End Times, you can incorporate Beautycounter's Brightening Facial Oil, which turns my dry party-streamer skin into a dewy, youthful lie. The founder, Gregg Renfrew (A WOMAN, CALM DOWN!), was furious about the shit ingredients in cosmetics, so she started her own company, which is not only lady run but also a certified B beauty corporation. Beautycounter also functions as a Mary Kay for millennials, meaning you can buy products from your bestie, and then she has a little extra scratch to buy you a vodka tonic. Closed female monetary system. Hallelujah.

TINTED MOISTURIZER

I used to use NARS tinted moisturizer with sunscreen, but they're dead to me now! I've switched to women-owned, cruelty-free Juice Beauty CC cream. It smells like a dandelion stem and makes my skin glisten like a beautiful sea snail.

EYE SHADOW (REGULAR LIFE)

I was using NARS, but again, fuck those dudes, so I switched to Melt. Co-founders Lora Arellano and Dana Bomar look like two women dancing at a St. Vincent concert that you stare at with your mushroomed-out eyeballs as a tear falls down your face because you are not friends with them.

EYE SHADOW (IMPRESSING OTHER WOMEN)

I was using Stila (Estée Lauder) Glitter & Glow liquid eye color but now I bedazzle my lids with Anna Petrosian's DOSE of COLORS. When you go out with sparkly eyelids, women WILL ASK you what eye shadow you're wearing and you have to be a good brand ambassador for the cosmetics ladies out there changing the ratio. Spread the good word, Janice Appleseed!

CONCEALER

I was using BECCA until I discovered they, too, are owned by Estée Lauder. I need a good concealer because my neighbors fuck really loudly to Portishead and I'm a light sleeper, which means every morning I wake up with purple circles under my eyes. Coupled with my paper-thin Irish skin, I look like the walking dead without concealer. I really like RMS Beauty's Beauty Un-cover up concealer. They sell at Sephora, but Sephora is dude-run, so color match there, put your fingers in all the products, swatch your face like a flesh rainbow, steal some register tape, scream "FIGHT THE PATRIARCHY," and then go to the RMS site to purchase.

MASCARA

I used to be dedicated to Laura Mercier's long-lash mascara, but then I got pinkeye and was like "fuck spending all this money on mascara" and bought this brand called Prestige, which I've since dumped for NUDESTIX vegan mascara. Started by two teenage sisters, this company also makes one-color face sticks for people like me whose personal brand[7] dictates all-over, monochromatic, "Yes, I made this macramé chandelier myself" desert author look.

BLUSH

Again, I owned every single NARS blush. I wish I could say it was joyful to throw them in the trash, knowing they'd be replaced by products I could feel better about, but the only solace I got was knowing a lot of them were ten years old and filled with pestilent microbial megacities. I switched to MAKE's Satin Finish Powder Blush in Geisha. It's the perfect utility blush color, PLUS the company gives 10 percent of its sales to We See Beauty, which then hands that money to women-

---

7   My personal brand is "lazy in neutrals."

led, worker-owned businesses, so you get two pussy points per purchase.

LIPSTICK

In 2015, Melissa Butler went on *Shark Tank* to pitch an idea—a natural lipstick that could be worn by every skin color without risking cancer tap dancing on your pie hole. The Sharks weren't buying it. Mr. Wonderful called her company, Lip Bar, "clown makeup" and said Butler and her crew were "colorful cockroaches." I would have poured nail polish remover all over the hood of Mr. Wonderful's Maybach, but class-act Melissa turned her time on *Shark Tank* into a business opportunity. Today, Lip Bar is thriving because women believed in her message, and her website reads like a women's studies class. On the "Lipbar 101" page she writes:

> I am passionate about creating an inclusive narrative on what beauty is and reminding women that we don't have to settle for anything. You are beautiful just the way you are. You don't have to transform to look like the next "It Girl." You don't have to do anything but be you, because you are enough.

Buy Lip Bar because their colors are amazing (and vegan) and it's a nice big "fuck you" to Kevin O'Leary.[8]

BROW FILLER

I once used Benefit, which I loved because they hired my first gay friend, Jade, to be a makeup artist at their Foley's counter. Jade is a petite man who moved from Bigot Grove, Texas, to be in Houston, which he thought would be a safer place. At the counter, I saw cowboys spit on him while walking through with their wives and the store did nothing about it. Benefit has a soft spot in my heart because of their counter-inclusiveness, but they're owned by Louis Vuitton, so now I use NUDESTIX Eyebrow Stylus Pencil.

PERFUME

I'll sometimes wear a shirt that's only staying out of the dirty clothes hamper because it vaguely smells like Le Labo Poivre 23. I figure I am ripping away thousands of dollars from men across the cosmetics

---

8 Kevin ran for head of the Conservative Party last year in Canada and might again, so I hope you're ready to see "Make Canada Great Again" hats.

universe, so maybe[9] you can rip my Le Labo out of my cold, dead hands.

It took me an entire plane ride from Boston to Los Angeles—SIX WHOLE HOURS, with the Gogo Internet actually functioning the whole time—to figure out which female-owned brands to give my beauty dollars to. When I was done, I felt a really deep sense of accomplishment. Look at me, I found out a way to make myself acceptably beautiful for society while making other women rich. When we were about to land, I was doing my face-cleaning remoisturizing routine and my mascara fell out of my makeup bag. The man next to me, who'd been watching old football games on ESPN Classic and smelled like Pringles farts, picked it up, handed it back to me, and said, "Here's your pen." After all my depressing research, if you told me he ran Urban Decay, I would have not been surprised.

---

9   As a poor kid, I always smelled like dust or old plastic shoes, so I am obsessed with smelling rich even if I haven't taken a shower in two days.

EMBRACE THE WOMAN YOU ARE, GIRL

In 2017, millions of people around the world came out to take part in the Women's March, and sure it was impactful or whatever, but I think it could've been more successful had they dropped the word *woman* and called it the "Girls' March." Everyone knows girls are the new women and women are the new decrepit, leather-faced, toothless forest witches.

Second-wave feminism was lousy with "women" women. In the '70s there was the Bionic Woman, Helen Reddy with "I am woman, hear me roar," and Enjoli,[1] the "eight-hour perfume for the twenty-four-hour woman." Women were everywhere, bossing

---

1   In full tilt commercial feminism, the jingle went "I can bring home the bacon, I can fry it up in a pan, and never ever let you forget you're a man. 'Cause I'm a woman." We *can* have it all! Work, cook, and fuck? *That's* what the Bionic Woman should've been about.

everyone around with their adult needs and opinions. It was exhausting taking all these women seriously. Thankfully, the Spice Girls kicked through a cotton candy wall and jumped over pink boa hurdles to save us all from them. They, along with Gwen Stefani and Beyoncé 1.0, gave us '90s Girl Power, punching the patriarchy in the face while eating ice cream in bright crop tops and brown lipstick. They weren't afraid to kick ass in a short skirt. But Girl Power wasn't a particularly feasible movement for me as a teenager. As someone who was five-nine in third grade, I've looked like a twenty-five-year-old Pottery Barn floor manager since elementary school. I didn't have time to stand up to my oppressors. I was too busy yanking down the girl-power babydoll dress so my vagina wouldn't touch the public school chairs. Girl Power fashion requirements didn't come in size "extra tall." The movement continued on without me and consumed everything in its path.

Girl, it's a girl's world now; women are just livin' in it.

What kind of girl are you, woman? It Girl? Daddy's Girl? Manic Pixie Dream Girl? Hollaback Girl? Party Girl? Working Girl? Gossip Girl? Mean Girl? Cash Me Ousside/Howbow Dah Girl? Maybe you're the kind of girl who wants to define what kind of girl she's grown up to be. Look at what a powerful movement Bethenny Frankel created as a skinny girl.

Skinnygirl margarita is the perfect cocktail for an innocent, carefree flirt. Doesn't that sound better than Skinny *Woman* margarita—perfect for an alcoholic in a stained nightshirt binging *Blue Bloods* at 3:00 p.m. on a Wednesday?

There's no shortage of girls to watch on TV: *2 Broke Girls*, *Gilmore Girls*, HBO's *Girls*, and *New Girl*—which is about a quirky "girl" in her thirties. A show called *New Woman* would be about a divorcée going to the dermatologist's office for a sobering talk about eczema.

When women go out, it's a *girl's* night out. The last girl's night out I had was with high school friends in Houston. We got tanked at a Vietnamese restaurant, well, all of us except for Gretchen, who had been sober since she'd landed in jail twice for drunk driving. Three hours later we were at Numbers (aka #'s), drinking well vodka and dancing to a Joy Division-heavy soundtrack. I got high in the bathroom with Carrie, who showed me her tummy tuck scar. So yeah, there's basically zero difference between that and a four-year-old girl's *Dora the Explorer*-themed birthday party.

It's relaxing to be a girl, because no one is trying to stomp on a girl's right to choose, 'cause the choice is nearly always strawberry. Girls don't have to be taken seriously, and when a girl accomplishes something it's more cute than impressive. Like all a girl graduating with a PhD in social work had to do was stand in front of a millennial pink wall, making a peace sign. Girls need protection and guidance. Women need Botox and Spanx.

But, girl, can we talk about girls in books? Girls TOTALLY RULE in books! Books with *Girl* in the title have been #1 *New York Times* best sellers for four out of the past six years. You know what books I'm talking about, girl: *Girl with the Dragon Tattoo, Girl on the Train, Gone Girl, The Girls, Some Girls, Razor Girl, The Good Girl, Girl in the Dark, Girls on Fire, Girl at War, Luckiest Girl Alive, The Girl Who Fell from the Sky, How to Build a Girl, A Girl Is a Half-Formed Thing.* One girl book explodes onto the scene and everyone wants to capture that magic. The magic being that a girl character raises the stakes. A dead girl has lost all her potential. A dead woman just loses her extensions.

But, according to FiveThirtyEight, the "girl" mentioned in the title of a book is much more likely to be a woman—titles featuring the word *girl* have spiked since the '90s (and especially since 2012, when *Gone Girl* debuted) and a full two-thirds of these innocent babes are actually full-on ladies. Sneaky bastards! The website also found if the title was written by a dude, the "girl" was more likely to end up dead. (If you're reading this right now, Robert Durst, STOP MASTURBATING!) Female authors are more likely to write books with *girl* in the title, although it's slightly unfair to put the blame on them because the title of a book is often a compromise between publisher and author. For example, I wanted to call this book *You're the Girl Now, Dawg* but they said the title "wasn't good" and to "return my advance." My publisher is missing out on MILLIONS because some exhausted Acuvue rep isn't picking up this book at a Denver International[2] bookstore because it doesn't have the word *girl* in the title!

When girl books hit pay dirt, Hollywood comes knocking, wanting to cash in on that sweet, sweet girl money. If I set foot in a movie theater for a girl-titled movie and the main character is a female in a tuckable turtleneck, I am asking to the see the manager. "Ma'am, are you aware the *girl* in this movie is a forty-five-year-old divorcée with visible gray roots? I'll take my $16 back please, plus parking. But I'm happy to pay for the Sour Patch Kids. At least *they* were as young as advertised."

It's not culturally acceptable to call a grown man "boy," unless you're already BFFs. I've never called my doctor up and asked, "Hey, boy, what did my blood panel say?" There's only one exception of a

---

2 If you ever have the pleasure to have an extra hour to kill at DEN, check out their death art. Whale extension, chemical warfare, mass murder, statues of demons in suitcases, everything you need to de-stress before your connecting flight.

boy label men would accept proudly: "bad boy." You know, the kind of guy straight women/gay men are not supposed to want but you just gotta have? A leather-clad motorcycle boy who ignores your "no shoes" rules and wears his dirty Frye boots all over your vintage rug. This boy knows what you want and he's gonna give it to you. Bad boys are so bad, Michael Bay was like, sign me up! I need the hottest bad boys!! *Ring ring.*

> *Michael Bay:* Hi, Will Smith and Martin Lawrence?
>
> *Will Smith + Martin Lawrence* (talking simultaneously): This is.
>
> *Michael Bay:* I just pulled a bunch of random pieces of paper out of my Dodgers cap and put them together on my marble coffee table. You know, the way I write all my movies. How does starring in a movie about "guns, explosions, heroin, and badass detectives" called *Bad Boys* sound?
>
> *Will Smith + Michael Lawrence:* Can we make three of them?
>
> *Michael Bay:* Uh, DOY!
>
> *Will Smith:* And can you make me seem happy?

The label "bad boy" elicits power and independence. Drop the "bad" and it becomes less appealing to many men. Foghorn Leghorn Southern racists use "boy" to demean. These cartoon antebellum torch-carriers use the word quickly to assert the dominant position, and you best not disrespect them the same way. In 2012, I was doing this experiment where I would call anyone, regardless of gender, "girl." Most people in LA loved it, probably because I sold it with a tone of "we don't know each other, but I like you." (Also, most people in LA would be happy if you called them prepubescent because it confirms their skin care routine is working.) Then I went to the Democratic National Convention[3] in Bathroom Bill Ground Zero, North Carolina. It was rainy, but security wasn't letting people take their umbrellas inside. (Even the DNC is on to the Penguin's revenge capers.) I set down my travel umbrella, which I'd owned for six years and was part of my family due to my unhealthy attachment to inanimate objects. Then I went inside where a bunch of politicians were preaching to the choir. After the event, I realized thousands of people had also left their umbrellas in my spot, all of whom were in a hurry to get

---

3 While I was there, I offered Jared Leto a cookie and he did not take it. It's not at all important to this story, but it is important that you know that Jared Leto will ignore your chocolate chip cookie offer even if you're in the VIP box as a guest, and repeatedly assure him you're not a crasher. I want him to know I was being sincere and I will never, ever forgive him.

drunk ASAP, and I sure as hell wasn't going to let my precious parasol get lost in the stampede. A stout Michael Chiklis–adjacent police officer must've thought it was adorable that a grown woman in a dress would dig through a garbage pile of wet umbrellas and offered to help me look for my little baby. Five minutes later, I shoved my rain protector in his face and said, "Girl! I found it!"

His face turned so red I thought cartoon steam was going to shoot out of his ears. He was trying to keep his calm, but was barely hanging on.

"What did you call me?"

The police down South like to lock you up for lookin' at them wrong, and I had just done the language equivalent of reaching for his gun. He didn't have a reason to take me to jail, but Southern cops don't need a reason. I smiled at him and said, "I called you girl. What's wrong with being called 'girl'?" He bored a hole through my head with his cop eyes and I ran away before he could arrest me for sassing him twice.

Maybe I ran away too fast. Is it possible he wasn't mad I called him "girl" but mad that I called any adult "girl"? Maybe he wanted to sit me down and tell me "no woman should stand for that kind of treatment," but I doubt it. I'm pretty sure his idea of "woke" is pounding a cup of coffee to rev up his morning.

If he were a woman, I'd understand why he'd take offense. Calling a twenty-nine-year-old woman "girl" might seem like a compliment, but it's wrapped in a smallpox blanket of insults. It paints us as childish and makes our opinions easier to dismiss because inside we're just a six-year-old missing our front teeth with undiagnosable chronic nosebleeds. Calling a woman "girl" takes away everything we've worked for as adults, like our 401K and the $600 in it. Which wasn't easy to do over the course of ten years!

Corporations never got this memo, apparently. They believe girls are more symbolically powerful than women, which is why they rely on them when they're trying to make social statements. On March 8, 2017, a bronze statue of a young woman appeared in front of the Wall Street bull. *Fearless Girl* was commissioned by an investment company called State Street Global Advisors. The statue's placard reads, "Know the power of women in leadership. SHE makes a difference." SHE is capitalized because it's a reference to a gender-diverse fund run by State Street Global Advisors so people who care about diverse boards can invest in those companies. The best way I can describe it is if NASCAR races were one hundred ninety-nine laps of vertebrae-fracturing crashes and one lap of white wine drinking and discussion of *The Piano Teacher*. With the statue, State Street got to shout to the world, "HEY, THERE

AREN'T ENOUGH WOMEN ON COMPANY BOARDS!!!" The company itself has been putting heavy pressure on the businesses they boss around to diversify their lady-less corporate boards. That's a herculean effort considering Wall Street men seem to respond to directives with a shrug and a smarmy laugh. State Street took bold action. They voted down directors on boards they controlled that did not have women. Yes, mama! Drag that skeleton man out of the boardroom as he's clinging on to the gold-plated casters on his antiqued brown leather office chair! But as direct as they've been in exerting pressure on a business level, when it came to their corporate street art, they wanted something softer.

State Street Global's CEO Ron O'Hanley told the *Atlantic*, "With the statue, we were very focused on wanting to send the right message. The artist, Kristen Visbal, was terrific in trying to understand what this commission was really about. Early renditions had a more confrontational pose. But the point was not 'You versus me.'"

The artist herself echoed the nonthreatening tone the statue was meant to evoke. She told press this about *Fearless Girl*: "She is proud, but not confrontational."

I don't know what's not confrontational about *Fearless Girl*. Created in the image of a preteen girl, she's a four-foot, 250-pound statue, powerstancing—legs sturdy and wide, fists on her hips, poker face, standing strong against the wind and Wall Street's *Charging Bull*. She looks like off-duty Chloe Grace Moretz in *Kick-Ass*. Like at any moment she'd grab a double-sided katana and cut you in half while blowing a bubble. The only thing not confrontational about her is she doesn't have secondary sex characteristics. Had State Street Global[4] surprised the city with a bronze statue of a thirty-four-year-old woman in the same pose, she would have looked like a dick-stomping feminist, demanding the bull work on his rage issues.

Elizabeth Warren posed by *Fearless Girl* and tweeted the photo with the caption, "Fight like a girl." I get the symbolic gesture here—boys insult each other by saying "You fight like a girl" and we're saying there's nothing wrong with fighting like a girl. But there is. I don't want to fight like a girl and I don't want to fight like a boy. Children are weak. Have you ever been punched by a nine-year-old? It's like getting jabbed with a raw chicken wing. It's not intimidating. I want to fight like Linda Hamilton in *Terminator 2*. I want to flip my psych ward bed on its side and do one million pull-ups until my muscles

---

4   The needle is moving. According to the Gender Diversity Index, one-third of board seats went to women in the first quarter of 2018. At this pace, we'll reach gender parity on boards in 2055. For an industry that's so immediately reactive to the whims of imaginary numbers, I'm pretty sure they have it in them to move much faster on this issue.

are so bulging Madonna puts a picture of me on *her* fridge for #fitspo.

I get why people like the idea of girlhood. Girls twirl in lavender fields and have their whole lives ahead of them. That's more fun to think about than a damaged adult hobbling joylessly toward death. But women don't need a million reminders that our youth is the only currency we have in this world. And unless you and I are close enough that you've seen me naked in the Bloomingdale's dressing room, you don't get to call me girl.

I'm a *woman* who never misses a car payment, makes her own chicken stock, raises a beautiful (very reactive, somewhat territorial) terrier mix, drinks rosé over $20, and gives her husband blow jobs while wearing an Invisalign retainer.

'Cause that's what a woman does.

PUTTING THE "STEM" BACK IN FEMINISTEM

Allow me to ruin a national hero for you.

John Glenn was an asshole. ICYMI, he was the first American to orbit Earth, but that's not why he's a fleshbag full of giraffe turds.[1] John Glenn is a cum basket because, in 1962, he actively campaigned Congress to prohibit women from going into space. He took time out of his busy space career farting into space suits and not dealing with his T-zone issues to stop Jerrie Cobb—aerospace's Sandra Day O'Connor—from sharing in his galactic glory. Jerrie was a female pilot and one of the Mercury 13,[2] a group of thirteen women tested by the privately

---

1   Although I bet he got real cocky after he became a national hero. "What do you mean my table isn't ready, Olive Garden? I'm John MOTHERFUCKING SPACE LORD Glenn!"

2   Another of them being Jane Hart, a mother of eight in her forties.

funded Lovelace Foundation's Women in Space Program. They underwent all the same testing as the Mercury Seven and, in some cases, scored better than the men. Jerrie petitioned the House Committee on Science and Astronautics to let her go, but John Glenn had a strict "No Bitches in Space" rule. He told the panel:

> The men go off and fight the wars and fly the airplanes and come back and help design and build and test them. The fact that women are not in this field is a fact of our social order.

Wow. John Glenn is so sexist he makes Jerry Lewis look like Betty Friedan. His favorite justification for barring women from space was NASA's rule requiring astronauts to be jet pilots, a career women weren't allowed to pursue until 1976. But joke's on America; John Glenn didn't care about NASA's rules. If he did, he wouldn't have allowed himself to be an astronaut because he hadn't earned the science degree required by NASA to be one. John Glenn only had one rule for going into space: Have a prostate.

In 1963, a year after American Hero John Glenn curb-stomped women's dreams of going to space, Russia announced it was #TimesUp on space sexism and sent their first woman into orbit, cosmonaut

Valentina Tereshkova. NASA responded to this historic moment by dismissing her voyage—longer than all the time collectively spent in space by American astronauts—as a stunt. No, a stunt is riding a BMX bike up a tree. Valentina Tereshkova wasn't trying to get a sick sponsorship from Mountain Dew; she was orbiting goddamned Earth!

Finally, in 1983, eleven years after the crimping iron was invented, America got around to sending their first woman into space. Sally Ride made American herstory, but not before a rocket booster full of sexist bullshit was fired directly into her face: While prepping for her mission, NASA asked her if one hundred tampons would be enough for her seven-day mission. ONE HUNDRED TAMPONS. If a hundred tampons is not enough, someone get Sally Ride to the emergency room because she is DYING!

The battle for equality at NASA has been tough, but strides have been made. Half the graduating class in 2016 were female astronauts. But they might be the last. Self-contained human centipede Donald Trump plans to cut NASA's education wing entirely, which has historically sparked the inner science and engineering nerds in young girls. Before this NASA program, the only way to inspire women to pursue STEM (science, technology, engineering, and math) careers was to watch Dr. Dana Scully fight off an inside-out skin man with a defibrillator on *The X-*

Files. (This is a real thing called "the Scully Effect.") The Geena Davis Institute on Gender[3] in Media interviewed women in STEM and found two-thirds of them saw Gillian Anderson's character as a major role model. I get it. Dana Scully is the reason I chopped off my long hair, dyed it red, and committed to a sensible neutral palette of sleeveless turtlenecks my freshman year of college. But with the FBI forensic pathologist who carries extraterrestrial DNA leaving *The X-Files* reboot in 2018 and Trump's axing of NASA's education budget, how will we ever fix the gender imbalance in STEM?

According to Catalyst, only 24 percent of STEM jobs are held by women. That's the same percentage of people who enjoyed *Speed 2: Cruise Control!* When you get granular, the percentages dip real low. According to the National Science Foundation, women make up only 7.9 percent of mechanical engineers and 11.1 percent of physicists.

There's an argument that women aren't interested in these careers, to which I say "horse diarrhea." Of course women are interested in STEM careers! We're interested in everything. Some women love these things so much, they're willing to climb over a

---

3   When I have enough clout to open my own institute, I'll call it the "Erin Gibson Institute for Fashionable Size 11 Shoes." It will be filled with amazing shoes that look good on all Godzilla feet and I hope to see you there, Tyra and Uma.

ton of barriers to pursue them. In 2015, two female researchers decided to look into how gender affects the ability of PhDs to find postdoc jobs in life sciences. Dr. Fiona Ingleby and Megan Head talked to 244 people with biology PhDs and concluded that—surprise!!—there's a lot gender bias in academia. So they wrote a manuscript about it and submitted it to PLOS One, an online science resource/ spellcheck heart attack. The way it works in science journals is, in order for your article to be printed, it has to be approved by other people in your field. If those strangers don't think your shit is quality, they send it back to you with notes on how to do better, dummy. Then you fix your mistakes and resubmit it for consideration. Ingleby and Head[4] weren't published, because their anonymous peer reviewer had a problem with the way they interpreted their data. Anonymous Peer (whose gender we don't know but can guess!) took issue with the wild conclusion that women biologists were treated unfairly even though their research showed female doctoral candidates coauthored fewer papers. Anonymous Peer hypothesized women coauthored fewer papers because male doctoral candidates were able to work fifteen min-

---

4   Who should absolutely consider opening a detective agency with last names like that. Ingleby and Head—Dickless Tracys at your service.

utes longer per week, according to some study he did not reference, but did chalk up "marginal gender differences of physiology and health." If we're just throwing "what-ifs" around, let's say men *can* work for an extra fifteen minutes. Maybe their hands are more nimble and fresh because they're not exhausting them folding clean laundry until 11:00 p.m. Anonymous Peer also suggested "male doctoral students can probably run a mile race a bit faster than female doctoral students." Huh? Is there some Newtonian law I don't know about correlating paper writing and running? Anonymous Peer suggested a way to fix the manuscript would be for the women to find "one or two male biologists" to coauthor and help them strengthen it. What are they supposed to do with that criticism? Douse their work with Axe Body Spray and send it back in for reassessment? Or, maybe, Anonymous Peer, you just proved their point.[5]

Sexism in science can be so pervasive it infects female academics. Dr. Alice Huang is a seventy-eight-year-old female molecular biologist who writes an advice column for the journal *Science*. In

---

5 Q: How does this dude find the time to peer review when he spends 100 hours a week between complaining about the all-female *Ghostbusters* reboot, protesting outside of women-only coworking spaces, and jerking off into a rock-stiff sock? A: His God-given extra male minutes.

2015, she received a letter from a postdoc whose adviser, she said, had a habit of looking down her shirt during meetings.

Here's Dr. Huang's advice:

> Some definitions of sexual harassment do include inappropriate looking or staring, especially when it's repeated to the point where the workplace becomes inhospitable. Has it reached that point? I don't mean to suggest that leering is appropriate workplace behavior—it isn't—but it is human and up to a point, I think, forgivable.

Great news for me! If acting on your human impulses is forgivable, I'm going to start shitting wherever I want. I'm gonna go right into Chico's and, when the saleswoman asks if she can help me, I'll respond, "I'm here for a chunky necklace.[6] But first, nature calls!" And then I'm going to squat down on their faux marble floors and go to town. And when the security guard tries to drag me out, I'll scream, "IT'S HUMAN AND FORGIVABLE!"

Dr. Huang went on to tell this woman, who is dealing with a very unprofessional situation, "As

---

6 You never know who's gonna be wearing the chunky necklace in this book! It could be anyone!

long as your adviser does not move on to other advances, I suggest you put up with it, with good humor if you can."

Here's how you can handle it with humor. Next time a man is looking at your tits, try this: Look them in the eyes, giggle lightly, and say—loudly—"It's so funny that you're trying to look at my boobs!" Now you've got everyone's attention. Escalate your laugh into a deep, maniacal cackle. He'll try to leave the area, but you block him with your laugh-scream and shout, "It's so funny that you're trying to see my titties, 'CAUSE YOU'RE NEVER GONNA SEE THEM. EVVVVVVEEEEEEERRRRRRR!! AHA-HAHAHAHAHAHAHAHAHAAHAHAHAHA!!" And then you keep laughing until no one knows what to do so they pack up their things and leave the building out of fear for their own safety.

It's easy to villainize Dr. Huang, but when you look at her work—not only in science, but also in her work toward "the inclusion, development, and advancement of women in careers in microbiology"[7]— it makes me wonder what kind of bullshit she's been dealing with for the last fifty-one years. Women pur-

---

7   Given to her by the American Society for Microbiology, the oldest life science organization in the world. Their Twitter is full of posts like "Further support that prioinflammatory cytokines may contribute to cerebral malarial pathogenesis." I now read their feed when I can't sleep.

suing the careers of their dreams develop special rules to deal with the hostility around them—either because they think no one will do anything about the bad behavior (they usually don't) or because they don't have the energy to fight it. There are so many things to fight. And people. Like ex–University of Arizona astronomy professor Timothy Frederick Slater, who openly commented on women's bodies, went to strip clubs, and gave a student a vibrator shaped like a cucumber. Outside of being extremely inappropriate, it's a terribly cartoonish view of female sexual habits. I don't know any woman who has blasted salad ingredients up her vagina. We're not living in pioneer times where women masturbate with whatever bounty Mother Nature has provided for us. Maybe the butt end of a Sonicare or a heavy pressure hand shower, but not a cucumber. Never a cucumber.

And none of this was made public for over a decade until Timothy "A Pickle for Your Vagina" Slater was outed on the floor of Congress by Representative Jackie Speier.[8] In the meantime, he

---

8 Get to know Jackie Speier. United States congresswoman, reps California's Fourteenth District, aka Silicon Valley and southern parts of San Francisco. Honey, she's doing everything right. Has a train named after her for making commuter transportation better. In 1978 this bitch goes on a trip to investigate the site of the Jonestown Massacre. Like purple Kool-Aid Guyana Jonestown. 'Cause she thinks if she doesn't go, it'll be

moved from the University of Arizona to the University of Wyoming, where I bet no one knew his reputation for being an inappropriate dicksnot. Shuffling these male offenders from university to university accomplishes nothing. These guys need to LEARN! Maybe they can figure out a place to get some helpful information at the MASSIVE EDUCATIONAL FACILITIES they work at. Where's the mandatory "How to Not Harass the Females Around You" class these guys are required to take so they can be aware *of* their behavior and *why* it's unacceptable?

What happens when universities take the side of the harasser? Geoff Marcy, the world-renowned astronomer at UC Berkeley, sexually harassed so many women, female postdocs refused to apply for faculty positions at the college because they didn't want to

---

a step back for other women in politics! When they get there? Ambushed. She's shot five times, left for dead. Honey, she SURVIVES. Like a lady Jason Bourne. Time to crank out a memoir and kick it in Mexico for the rest of her life, right? Nah! This bitch runs for office. Fights for prison reform. Spends a night in jail just to see the conditions. Method honey! Works her way up to the U.S. House of Representatives. TIRELESS champion for gun control. Now look at her. Urging Congress to investigate the Russian hacking. She's working on making sharing revenge porn a crime and proposed two bills to prevent sexual harassment and abuse in academia. You even think about a vag in a sketchy way? Jackie takes off her earrings, leaps down ten stories, runs across rooftops spiked with glass, throat-kicks you, then PUTS THE EARRINGS BACK ON!

deal with his unwanted kissing, massaging, or worse—him grabbing their vaginas under tables at professional dinners.

Despite the accusations of many women,[9] UC Berkeley chose not to fire him. But because of the outrage online, Marcy resigned, issuing a perfect non-pology. "Non-pology" is a made-up word I use to describe a fake apology that acknowledges the *reaction* to the wrongdoing while *avoiding blame* for doing the bad thing in the first place. Here's Marcy's to illustrate:

> While I do not agree with each complaint that was made, it is clear that my behavior was unwelcomed by some women. It is difficult to express how painful it is for me to realize that I was a source of distress for any of my women colleagues, however unintentional.

In other words, "I'm sorry about your reaction to an innocent mistake outside of my control." I have a hypothesis for male scientists that I think will help them understand: *If* a woman is offended by your words, *then* you are saying something repugnant.

When you read about the next guy, you're gonna wonder why we let these dudes near explosive

---

9   This number SHOULD be 1.

lab equipment. Tim Hunt, a Nobel Laureate bio-chemist from the redundantly named University College London, was speaking at the World Conference of Science Journalists in South Korea, specifically addressing a convention of senior female scientists and science journalists. And here's what he said to an audience of women. "Let me tell you the trouble with girls[10]...three things happen when they are in the lab: You fall in love with them, they fall in love with you, and when you criticise them, they cry."

Way to know your audience, Tim! Follow it up with your tight five on Korean comfort women! After his speech, Tim flew home, trudged up to his office, pulled out a skeleton key—or whatever British people unlock doors with—and packed up all his stuff because he was forced to resign. For anyone who feels like these guys shouldn't lose their jobs or step down, take that sympathy, box it up, wrap it, put a bow on it, and hand it over to the women who were pussy-shoved out of their science careers. Or fired for just being a woman who dared to exist in the company of men.

Scientists starting their careers depend exclusively on the favor of faculty members above them

---

10   "Women," not "girls," Tim.

for everything. If you have a serial harasser who's the only person with the power to give you access to research funding and you know your college won't do anything about his advances, it doesn't take a scientist to deduce the two possible outcomes are "dreadful" and "horrible."

The Center for Talent Innovation—an advocacy group focused on diversifying the workforce—did a study on STEM careers with cry-worthy results. When the report asked senior STEM leaders—both men and women—if they thought a woman would be able to reach top jobs at their organization, a third of them plainly said no. As if that weren't terrible enough, women are paid $58,000 compared to men with the same degrees who are bringing home $85,000. Which is weirdly like someone in the payroll department going, "How can we streamline our gender pay gap? I know…we'll just switch around the first two numbers!"

And if you're a black or Hispanic woman, the science world could at least pat you on the head and say, "It's so sweet you think you can do this. Bless your heart!" That would be *nicer* than how those fields currently treat these women. In a study by UC Hastings, 100 percent of the women of color reported gender bias. ALL OF THEM! There wasn't one woman of color in science in this study who reported her career was "smooth sailing."

"You always have to prove yourself...to show skill. I've never, ever had anything easy," one black biochemist told UC Hastings. Latinas, meanwhile, were more likely to be asked by male colleagues to do admin work like organizing meetings and filling out forms. According to the study Double Jeopardy,[11] authored by three distinguished female professors (and coauthored by zero men), nearly half of the black and Latina scientists said they were REGULARLY MISTAKEN AS JANITORS.

A statistician in the report said at first she chalked it up to her being at the lab at weird hours. She said, "They assume that I am the janitor, okay?...I always amuse my friends with my janitor stories, but it has happened, not only at weird hours."

Look, there is no shame in being a janitor. Some of the nicest alcoholics I know are janitors. But can you imagine going to school for seven hundred years, getting your dream job, and while you're at work, splicin' those genes, someone taps you on the shoulder and says, "Uh, we're out of toilet paper in the shitter. And Jason's been eating a lot of Chobani even though he's lactose intolerant...so it's rough in there."[12] It's rude and sexist, but also so stupid.

---

11 The study was so discouraging and sad, they were practically forced to name it after the lackluster 1999 Ashley Judd thriller.

12 Am I to believe that there are a ton of male scientists who see a woman holding an electron microscope and say to themselves,

Fixing this problem will require a veritable fuck-ton of work, but it'll pay off in spades. We need STEM journalists, STEM faculty, STEM mentors to make these fields safe for women to learn and thrive. We need more STEM women in positions of power. And if you are a university, use this rule from the Carl Sagan's Baloney Detection Kit—a practical guide for dealing with bullshit. It's one of my favorite rules, and the one I think every institution should use when considering the excuses of men in positions of power:

> Arguments from authority carry little weight— "authorities" have made mistakes in the past. They will do so again in the future.[13]

In the vein of being objective and rational—ya know, two basic SCIENTIFIC PRINCIPLES—we need ALL OF THE BRAINS on the science jobs building floating bridges, curing diseases, inventing 4D printing, solving the singularity, destroying Facebook, designing driverless cars that don't murder, all of it!

There's a reason I'm so passionate about having

"Okay, this is a tough one. She's either holding a piece of scientific equipment or a broom."

13 Wise words from a smart man who rocked a rust-colored turtle-neck like no one else.

more women in STEM. Number one, it's fair and just and all that stuff. Number two, and this is very personal, I need women on the job of figuring out proper dosages for pot brownies, which are wildly inconsistent. This is very serious. Figuring this out is the difference between me being at the airport, underneath a seat, crushed by the idea of infinite space and me joyfully dancing to "Bitch Better Have My Money," chompin' on some Shake Shack! Get your shit together, STEM, and let those women in! My travel experience depends on it!

THE NFL DOES NOT CARE ABOUT YOUR BREAST CANCER

If poor Irish families had coats of arms, ours would look like this: a griffin drunk on Jameson, a lion giving a fawn an Ogilvie home perm, a dragon cheating at Balderdash, and a wild boar riddled with breast cancer in all eight of its teats. What my family lacks in natural talents[1] we more than make up for in our ability to get breast cancer. Two aunts and a grandmother, all taken from us by the deadly tumors. My mom, two more of her sisters, and a cousin all successfully warded off breast cancer with chemotherapy. The rest of the women in the family wait for it to choose one of us. Who will be next? (Cue *Children of the Corn* music.)

---

1   Some of us can sing Bonnie Raitt songs fairly proficiently.

Breast cancer is scary. Not to say all cancers aren't scary, they are. But breast cancer has an added fear factor: the constant reminders of its existence. Remember the last time a trip to Target didn't involve walking past breast cancer awareness pink ribbon flip-flops, coloring books, batteries, spatulas, shower curtains, or dog bones? I don't. Target, to me, is just a bunch of breast cancer awareness products and a drapery aisle where all the panel curtains are only available in singles. Sorry about your wide living room window, Neely! Looks like your neighbor will be keeping her front-row view of your Saturday *Frasier* binge sessions. It's one thing to see a breast cancer awareness shaving cream next to your razor refills; it's another one to see it and be reminded of the thing that murdered your sweet fucking grandma.

"But, Erin," my mom says after she's given me a breast cancer awareness umbrella, "think about the lives this plastic garbage from China saved!"

"I don't know, Mom, but lung cancer is the number one cancer killer among women and I don't see anyone wearing a 'Save the airbags' T-shirt during Lungs Are Sexy fun runs," I tell her hours later when I have the energy to rehash the conversation on my own terms in a bathtub after googling cancer stats.

Why does breast cancer get to hog all the awareness? I've heard a rumor that everyone loves boobs.

But the obsession with jugs can't fuel the awareness machine entirely. I know plenty of guys who love big beautiful butts but I'd be hard-pressed to find someone passionate about curing ass cancer.

Breast cancer awareness is the invention of one of the largest manufacturers of the breast cancer drugs Arimidex, Imfinzi, Zoladex, Calquence, Iressa, Casodex, Lynparza, Falsodex, Tagrisso, and Nulbien. Just kidding. The last one I made up. What a ridiculous name for a serious drug! "National Breast Cancer Awareness Month is now a legacy program of the AstraZeneca[2] HealthCare Foundation," reads the description of the website run by the cancer drug king.

According to their website, www.beautifulcancerfreetits.org, just kidding, it's their name dot com, they made $6.9 billion dollars of core operating profit[3] in 2017. That's enough money to light cigars with flaming thousand-dollar bills—if those even exist. I'm not a money expert. As far as I'm concerned, the $50 U.S. savings bond I won in fifth grade will pay for my retirement. And I only google information allowing me to win arguments with my mother, so I guess we'll never know if thousand-dollar bills are a thing.

---

2   Do you think AstraZeneca is a beautiful name for a daughter conceived in the EDM tent at Coachella?

3   Earnings before interest and taxes are subtracted, for anyone who cares to know.

Call me a cynic, but the idea of a company profiting off breast cancer, then starting a charity to draw attention to breast cancer seems suspect. Imagine if Walter White had started a Meth Addiction Awareness Campaign to help people find out if they love meth. To me, breast cancer awareness is a money hustle for drug companies. And the hustle is catching on.

Breast Cancer Awareness Month used to just be October, a time to remind women to lay those boobs in between two below-freezing metal plates and let the machine that crushes old cars into neat little squares go to town on them. Personally, I'd rather be repeatedly punched in the tit than have a mammogram. During the procedure, I found it unbelievable that my breast tissue wasn't shooting out of my nipple. I had my first mammogram at twenty-eight, because of my family history of breast cancer, and you better believe I hated every minute of this very important, life-saving breast cancer screening.

But Breast Cancer Awareness, like, um, cancer, has spread to other months. And it's not just about cancer screenings; it's about SHOPPING! Sunglasses and lip balm and scarves and KFC chicken and candles and water bottles! Any product can be affiliated with breast cancer awareness! Take the NFL: Their approach to breast cancer awareness integration is like a fanatical mother planning her only daughter's first wedding. They slap Pantone 218 pink on everything—shoes, sweatbands, shirts, penalty flags. Thank you, sports group who can't seem to curb domestic abuse by the hands of your own players and grossly underpays cheerleaders. You do care about women! The other cool thing about the NFL's fundraising efforts is they're accountable to no one. While the LA Rams' New Era, heather-gray breast cancer awareness sideline hat will set you back $25.99, only a sliver will actually make it to charity. According to Julie DiCaro at *Sports Illustrated* (which I read for the very first time just to bring you this!), only $12.50 of every $100 of pink merchandise goes to the American Cancer Society (ACS) CHANGE program. This program awards grants to community-based health facilities located within a hundred miles of an NFL[4] city to *educate* women about breast health. It's breast cancer awareness awareness. Which I have now made you aware of, making it breast cancer awareness awareness awareness.

CHANGE said they answered seventy-two thousand women's questions about early detection of breast cancer. Wow! That's probably 1/1,000,000,000,000th of the times Google has answered the same questions. They also bragged about screening ten thousand

---

4   In 2017, the NFL broadened their awareness from just breast cancer to cancer. #allcancersmatter Now, if we can only get them to care about what Colin Kaepernick is saying...

women at little or no cost. "Little cost"? Shouldn't it be fucking free? Here's what they do, explained in this delicious word salad on their website:

> CHANGE grants serve as a catalyst for partners to implement and sustain interventions to effectively engage and mobilize patients; and implement systems and policies that are essential to increasing access to timely cancer screenings.

Women in underserved communities don't need a lesson in breast exams, a pamphlet, and a pat on the back; they need practical help that the American Cancer Society and the NFL are not providing. If breast cancer awareness were an actual philanthropic endeavor, 100 percent of the fund-raising would go toward research to find a cure (good luck, with drug companies making cigar-lighting profits) AND helping women who have breast cancer. The Pink Fund, a nonprofit providing financial assistance to women undergoing breast cancer treatment, conducted a study in 2017 and found that 41 percent of women skipped medication or treatment because of financial obstacles and 37 percent are in debt after treatment. This shit makes me so mad I want to kick my clog booties through the wall...but I own my home and it took me a long time to find a pair of Dutch-inspired footwear that didn't make me look like I'm wearing Optimus Prime Transformer feet, so I'll settle for screaming into a drool-stained pillow. There's absolutely no reason any woman should go into debt to stay alive when there is plenty of breast cancer money floating around to help them.

Time for some math! Get out your calculators and your graph paper and your eraser and your ruler and your protractor and your gin! Here's your SAT question: If the National Cancer Institute says they spent $519,000,000 on breast cancer research along with the National Institutes of Health which spent $656,000,000[5] and in Lea Goldman's *Marie Claire* article "The Big Business of Breast Cancer," she estimates $6 billion a year is raised by breast cancer awareness programs, how much money is breast cancer making? Take your time. My iPhone started doing this e9 shit, so I had to do the math the old-fashioned way: with a barely working mechanical pencil on the back of a laser hair removal pamphlet.

That's right! It's a whopping $7,175,000,000!

Okay, so let's set the average cost of chemotherapy to treat breast cancer at $30,000[6] and there are on average 230,000 women diagnosed yearly in the

---

5 Based on their 2016 budgets.
6 The actual cost can vary wildly, and this number is sort of in the middle. We can all agree anyone paying for medical care out-of-pocket would be able to put $30,000 to use immediately.

United States, which makes the cost of treating all the women with breast cancer diagnoses... $6,900,000,000, leaving a whopping $275 MILLION dollars for research! That's the real breast cancer awareness! Are you *aware* of how many women could be helped right now today this second who aren't 'cause it's all getting dumped into research and making shitty pink mouse pads?

Or maybe it's just getting straight-up wasted. One scummy organization, the Breast Cancer Society, was embroiled in a massive charity fraud case, reported on by Rebecca R. Ruiz in the *New York Times*, where the people running the group (and three other cancer charities) spent donations on being extra in so many ways, but specifically, eating at Hooters and shopping sprees at Victoria's Secret. WHAT HILARIOUS TRASH! Misappropriating breast cancer donations to buy things at boob places?!?

There are antebellum elevators I trust more than some of the charities associated with breast cancer. But breast cancer sleazes shouldn't deter you from doing everything you can to stay on top of your personal breast health. First of all, get acquainted with your boobs and do a monthly self-exam. Maybe time it after an evening spent watching Tom Hardy in *Warrior* or an hour lost on Michael B. Jordan's shirtless Instagram selfies. What I'm saying is, have fun with it. According to a study published by the American

Medical Association, having ten or more drinks a day can increase your risk, so don't work at a winery. Get those knockers squished. And if you think anything is wrong, demand to have the issue dealt with.

If you're me, and wonderful women you love have died from breast cancer, get genetic testing. When the test for the BRCA1 & BRCA2 gene came out, my mom begged Audrey and me to do it. The genes produce tumor suppressor proteins, and if these genes have a mutation on them, it gives you a 70 percent lifetime likelihood for getting boob cancer. The older you get, the higher your chances. Wish that was the rule for acting roles, right, ladies? #hollywoodjoke But those stats didn't scare me. I was twenty-eight and I had better things to worry about, like "Can I pull off skinny scarves?" Turns out the answer is no. Paired with a tank top, they make me look like *The Pirates of the Caribbean*'s accounts payable department.

To pacify my justifiably frightened mother, I got a mammogram (referenced above, boobs turned into papyrus by the cold metal hands of a robot). Turns out I have dense breasts, way up on every guy's list, right up there with "vascular butt." Dense breasts are hard to monitor, so I was off to my first breast MRI. They found nothing, but one of the technicians told me I'd probably have to do these screenings every year. My mom and her sisters spent their thirties getting lumpectomies, where a doctor opens your breast like a toaster oven and fishes out suspicious bumps, and so here I was, staring down the same road. It's not how I planned to spend my thirties. What about the time machine I wanted to build to travel back to 1996 and marry *Trainspotting*-era Ewan McGregor?

Audrey's results came back negative. She called to tell me the good news and ask me when I was getting the test done. I wasn't; I was very busy with 11:00 p.m. Tuesday night improv rehearsals for my comedy group Panties in a Bunch. WHY COULDN'T EVERYONE SEE HOW SWAMPED I WAS?! Then I get a call from her later that week. She was discussing my personal testing decisions with her genetic counselor and he said, "If you knew your sister was about to jump off a bridge, wouldn't you save her?" Who knew Houston genetic counselors were such drama whores? Take that scene-stealing energy to the Alley Theatre, right, Houston? #houstonjokes

The next week I was tested through the Gilda Radner[7] program at Cedars in Los Angeles. They called with the news a couple weeks later—I was carrying a GENETIC TIME BOMB. I started looking into my options for a double mastectomy. I saw a male oncologist who told me not to do it. Despite all the women

---

7   Gilda was an actress and comedian from *SNL* who died of ovarian cancer after being misdiagnosed for years. When she was finally diagnosed, she turned to her husband at the time, Gene Wilder, and said "Thank God, finally someone believes me!"

with breast cancer he'd seen die, he didn't see why I should have to have such a radical surgery at such a young age. I asked him if he'd ever seen a twenty-nine-year-old die of breast cancer, and he replied, "Yes, many." So he's seen women die at my age, but I shouldn't have the surgery because of some reason he wants to stay mysterious about? I didn't have a particular attachment to my teeny girls, Louisa May Alcott and Amelia Earhart; I was an A on a bloated day. I understand it must be harder for women with perfect tits to chop them off, but nothing is as important as being alive. And getting rid of your boobs does you a service. It's hard for the worst guys who are great at pretending they're the best guy to hide their disappointment when hearing the words *double mastectomy*. Any man whose jaw drops and color disappears from his cheeks doesn't deserve the pleasure of seeing you naked.

My terrible gynecologist (who I will talk about more in a later chapter) tried to talk me out of the double mastectomy, because "How would [I] breast-feed?" To which I replied, "Not very easily if I'm dead." In his eyes, boobs > women. Despite all these doctors who were spewing bad advice about my corrupted chest, I cut them off anyway…because I found out I could get bigger ones! Yeah, that's right. I had a preventive mastectomy for bigger boobs. If I'm gonna go through a bunch of surgery, there better be a fucking prize at the end!

Double mastectomies are not easy. They removed my breast tissue and axillary lymph nodes to be sure anything that might get cancer was gone. Then they threw my tainted body parts in the trash, I guess. I don't know what they do with them. Do they throw them in the garbage? Like, does some raccoon dive into a dumpster looking for four-day-old spaghetti only to find someone's useless discarded knee is on the menu? What I *do* know is some of my body trash went to a research program. And if I ever find out my cells are in some Henrietta Lacks situation where they're being used for profit by some medical corporation, especially AstraZeneca, I'm calling Gloria Allred and I'm SUING! And then I'm calling Emily Blunt and BEGGING HER TO PLAY ME IN THE MOVIE!

When I awoke in my hospital bed, I couldn't sit up because apparently you need your chest muscles to be upright. Mine were all fucked up from being crowbared off my ribs so an expander could be shoved underneath them. My blood pressure for the next five days was insanely low, so when the nurse tried to sit me up to eat, I could hear my heart pumping blood into my brain like a bass drum under my skull. There's no sleeping in the hospital either. Rest is the time you get taking naps between people coming in to make sure you're not dead. My mother was unable to handle the state I was in, which she expressed by nervously brushing the knots out of my nasty hair until my husband removed her from the room because she was hurting me.[8] I don't agree with my mother about looking your best when lying in a hospital bed with a catheter shoved up your ureter, smelling of BO and whatever antiseptic they washed your incisions with, but then again, my mom's sisters all died with fake lashes on, so maybe it's a generational thing.

It took me three weeks to sit up without getting light-headed. I slept on a pillow shaped like a triangle. Underneath my arms, where they took out lymph nodes, were two tubes going into my skin draining pus and blood and miscellaneous fluids from my wounds into a collection cup safety-pinned to my surgical wrap, which was as fascinating as it was disgusting. But it tasted surprisingly good. Just kidding. Sorry if I made you barf just now.

The most exciting days I had were when I could walk from my house to Skylight Books without passing out. The rest of the time I was at home watching *Kitchen Nightmares*, and I am not complaining about it! I could watch Gordon Ramsay scream at a binder clip and be entertained. Every couple of weeks I'd see my plastic surgeon, who would inject saline into my ex-

---

8 Sure could have used a husband intervening during those before-school morning ponytails. I can't be the only woman who had migraines from her ponytails being too tight in kindergarten. All roughhousing girls like myself should have Miley Cyrus *Wrecking Ball* haircuts.

panders to stretch out my pectoral muscles a little bit at a time so a big ol' B-cup implant could be popped right in. Once they were the right size, I went back in for the implants. It was outpatient surgery and my hair looked great. My boobs, on the other hand, looked okay. They're *very* round and sit very high up. They sort of look like two baked Alaskas with a nipple on top. Once I was healed enough, I tried sleeping on my stomach, which was the first time I cried. It was like lying on two hard rocks and all the nerves around my chest and underarms were shot from being cut apart and for what? It took me three months of healing and two surgeries and here I was a Frankenboob lady. All to be free of a cancer I didn't even have. The regret was overwhelming, and you don't get counseling on how to deal with this massive physical change when you're done with the surgeries. I was stuck trying to figure out how to move forward with these alien domes in my chest and I had no one to call because Angelina Jolie hadn't had her surgery yet and we aren't friends. But unsolicited advice was worse. No surprise there. Women telling me I should've gotten the teardrop implants; they looked more natural. Warning me not to do pushups because it would turn my implants square. They were already weird looking, why not up the ante and turn them into single-knobbed Legos?

I did do pushups and my boobs did not turn into

squares. I did everything I could to get back to normal: yoga, weightlifting, spin class, hamburgers. But I was better than "back to normal." I went into this journey with massive breast cancer risk and I left it with nearly zero. No more mammograms, no lumpectomies. Just smooth boob sailing…until I need to have my implants replaced per my doctor's recommendation. But then smooth sailing.

If you find yourself in a situation where you are being threatened by your ta-tas, don't save them; save yourself. Don't worry about who you are without them. Guys will miss putting their dick between them, but what if you could offer up something more exotic? When I was recovering on my triangle pillow and unable to sit up, my (now-ex)husband was so horny, but I didn't know how I could help him with his important problem. I thought about it for a long time and then I said, "Do you want to fuck my feet?" His eyes lit up like Shirley Temple in *The Little Princess* when she wakes up in the orphanage to kippers and satin robes set before her while she slept in her sad little cold attic room. Two pumps of his signature Nivea lotion and my pressed-together arches were a perfect dick catcher. Cancer free and still able to please my man with second-tier dick holes. Who am I? Wonder Woman?

WRITING A LETTER TO A PERSON YOU DISAGREE WITH TO MAKE THEM SEE HOW WRONG THEY ARE

!!WARNING!!

This chapter was written exclusively for secretary of education, Betsy Crocker[1] DeVos. I know it's not her style to read pieces by people like me—snowflake libtards who drown Christian fetuses in trans-friendly bathrooms—but I am pretty confident she will read this. Why? Because I Secreted it and the Secret is legitimate mind power used to will things into being, like money, and that's why I have $400 million. So, if your name is not Betsy DeVos, STOP READING!

(If your first name is Betsy, fine, I guess you can skim this chapter, but only if you take the information back to your network of Betsys.)

---

1   Her actual middle name according to me.

Dear Mrs. Betsy DeVos,

You don't know me, but I want to help you. It's big of me, I know, since you barely deserve it, but I am doing it because I want you to do a better job as secretary of education. And to do that, you need some information I just happen to know, through my dedication to politics, fairness, and skimming Twitter on the toilet. If you would allow it, dear madam, I would like to lay out some helpful information in very simple language, using references you'll understand. Go grab your multicolored Saks Fifth Avenue readers—you know, the bejeweled ones with the neck strap that jangles—and concentrate on what you're about to read, Betsy. Take notes in the margins. Read out loud if it helps (ain't no shame in being an auditory learner!). But take this very seriously. The well-being of young American women depends on it.

You know this already, but in case your Velcro curlers are constricting your memory, I wanted to remind you about a little not-so-sweet thing you did recently—you rolled back Obama-era campus rape guidelines. Obama—the last good president America never deserved—put these provisions in place specifically to do two things: help women in college who have been sexually assaulted seek help and prevent future sexual assault. Did you know women age eighteen to twenty-four are three to four times more likely to be sexually assaulted than women in any other age group? Yuh-huh! Which means if a sixteen-year-old girl's chance of being sexually assaulted is 20 percent, then her chances go up to 60 percent when she turns eighteen and goes to college. That's called "multiplication." Shockingly, I learned that in a publicly funded school! Publicly funded means paid for by taxes, which means Chipotle didn't sponsor my Spanish classes and Mountain Dew didn't own our water fountains.

Now, I know you *think* you did your homework before you took away these Obama-era protections. Look at you! You took meetings with rape survivor advocates and experts like the National Women's Law Center! They told you how these provisions were overdue and necessary so women could learn shit without the constant fear of being assaulted by a guy in flip-flops named Thad. Not being satisfied with the experts and firsthand testimonies, you took meetings with the angry blowhards on the other side. You spoke to men's rights activists, a group of "oppressed"[2] men channeling "my wife divorced me" anger into a movement weaponizing their sense of rejection. You spoke to the furious moms whose sons turned out to be asshole rapists when they sent them

---

2   It's like the old women's studies tramp stamp says, "When you're accustomed to privilege, equality feels like oppression."

off to UConn and don't think their wittle boys deserve to have their lives ruined just because they shoved their dicks into unsuspecting women. When you got into your Audi Quattro and prayed on who you should believe, Jesus whispered, "The rapists," and here we are.

Look, I get it, you're very wealthy and detached, and you'd probably rather be at a gala right now. Politics is hard and requires so much reading of things that aren't the Bible. It's exhausting, but at 6:00 p.m., thank God, you can put on your $3,000 Barbour wax jacket and hide in the gaudy McMansion your Amway fortune affords you as a member of the Grand Rapids elite.[3] You can put your feet up and wrap your lips around canapés in silence because you *will* fire staff if they speak after sundown. You can retreat to your own weird world and not have to think about the big bad men and what they do to women. It would be easy to blame your lack of empathy on the oil-baron circles in which you run, but I won't do that. There's a bigger problem outside of the lopsided income distribution in this country that allows rich people to check out of social issues affecting most Americans. The problem is information. Though the mere mention of the word makes your already exhausted neurons work triple-

---

3   Which I assume is you, your husband, Amway Jr., and whoever owns the most Quiznos franchises in town.

time, hear me out. The sad fact is, while we're drowning in studies on why women are the victims of sex crimes, we've got a limited few on why men commit the crimes. So, it's understandable why someone like you would be so confused about rape statistics. How can we stop a crime if we don't know who is doing it and why? We can't, Betsy.

Betsy?

Betsy?!

Betsy!!!!!

Put down *Farmville* on your iPad, please. This is important!

I know you don't read the failing *New York Times*,[4] so I'll tell you about an eye-opening article I read by Heather Murphy called "What Experts Know About Men Who Rape." In it, she talks to Sherry Hamby, the editor of *Psychology of Violence*, the only American Psychiatric Association journal I give to children for their birthday.

Hamby says for every ten study submissions she receives about victims, she gets only one on perpetrators. Why is that? Because even in social science, the idea that women are somehow responsible for the things happening has seeped in.

The data social scientists *do* have is very limited.

---

4   To be honest, after that Nazi sympathizer article, if I see a white male byline, I throw my laptop into rush-hour traffic.

But, thankfully, one or two scientists took time out of their busy schedules to pursue this information with the same sort of dedication you put into squeezing as many windows into your lakeside mansion as possible. (Why does it look like your architect, Poor Man's Frank Gehry, glued one hundred Home Depot windows together instead of building a single curved pane of glass on your second-story sunroom? You have the pyramid scheme [excuse me, "multi-level marketing opportunity"] fortune to afford[5] a beautiful house, Betsy!)

As much as I would like to slap your architect in the face for constructing a mansion that looks like the fever dream of a hobbit who just won the lottery, this is not an intervention about your design aesthetic. This is about stopping campus assault. And here's how we do it. Like a pioneer wife left alone in her winter cabin to fend for herself, armed with nothing but a shotgun, a match, and a bag of flour, we must make do with what we have. And here it is.

The idea people have of a rapist is much different from the reality of who actually rapes. Unlike what you think, Betsy, they aren't dirty men with vampire teeth, salivating from behind a bush with a boner in their farm overalls. According to Lawrence Green-

---

5 Money can buy you class if you can admit you have none in the first place and hire someone to have it for you.

field's 1997[6] report on rape and sexual assault for the U.S. Department of Justice, they found close to 99 percent of sexual assaults are perpetrated by men, and six out of ten are white. Sexual predators can literally be anyone—male comedians, current and past U.S. presidents, morning show hosts, liberal politicians, Civil Rights heroes, and pebble-faced blob-cock men building their film production empires off of Uma Thurman's talent. And those are just the famous people! You said in a speech to Congress, "There are men and women, boys and girls, who are survivors, and there are men and women, boys and girls, who are wrongfully accused." But very, very few people have been falsely accused and convicted for a rape they didn't commit. According to the National Registry of Exonerations, since 1952, there have been only fifty-two cases where men convicted of sexual assault were exonerated.

What's far more likely to happen is that rapists never have to face the consequences of their actions. According to RAINN (Rape, Abuse & Incest National Network), out of 1,000 rapes, 994 perpetrators will walk free. And these sexual predators could be people you know, Betsy—your heavily armed limo

---

6 Now, I know the data is old (but not that old, right Cypress Falls High School Class of '97—Go Eagles!!), but again, so few people are willing to dive into the mind of a rape-y man to learn more.

driver, your spray-tanner, maybe even the Pizza Hut rep hocking your charter school edible cheesy breadstick–branded textbooks. These are guys most people would consider "normal." Guys who stop at stop signs, who send their moms birthday cards and pay their taxes.

Many of these rapists start in high school or college, according to research cited in Murphy's *New York Times* article. In contrast to honing skills like playing the violin or perfectly blowing out a cowlick, sexual predation expertise takes relatively little time to develop.

These young men fine-tune their skills on people they know—a girlfriend, someone they've been flirting with at a party, a coworker at the college library. One day you're just hanging out with your friend Jimothy,[7] toolin' on how many dorks are reading *Ready Player One*, and the next day he pulls you into the reference stacks and shoves his slimy Gatorade tongue down your throat.

Don't feel bad for Jimothy's[8] future, Betsy! According to social psychologist Antonia Abbey, there's hope he won't continue to be a Great Dane turd wrapped in Billabong gear. If Jimothy regrets touch-

---

7   A real name of a real dog I know in Los Angeles.
8   Low odds you were feeling bad for the woman in this scenario, Betsy.

ing a female butt without permission, he'll stop the behavior and give up a life of being a menace to women. Jimothy will thus prove he was born with enough empathy and understanding of human decency to realize the impact his actions have had on other people. But if Jimothy doesn't feel bad, he'll keep touching women without consent. Jimothy will slowly turn into the kind of man who thinks of women as "fuck holes." As human property for the taking, as it is written in the Bible.

But if you asked Jimothy, he wouldn't see his actions as assault. He would have tons of excuses straight out of *Rape, It's Not Your Fault: A Survival Guide for Rapists.* The most classic excuse is that somehow the victim deserved it. The idea being that women can send out arousal messages only men can hear, so how could a rapist be responsible for following *her* orders?

There are a lot of secret messages women can send—with the way we walk and smile, the raspy voices we get after the flu, eating a refreshing ice cream cone, taking our hair out of a ponytail after spin class to see if it looks beachy or nasty. But the number one way people think women secretly give men imaginary permission to touch us is by the way we dress. Specifically, when we dress "sexy."

Sexy is subjective. How am I supposed to know what's "sexy" to every man on planet Earth? I think

I look fucking hot in a blousy black turtleneck, sporting deadstock two-tone '70s-era Michael Caine glasses, my filthy, dandruff-y hair reeking of dry shampoo thrown into a lazy bun. According to rapists' logic—before I set foot outside my door, I have to evaluate whether that very specific outfit might trigger a hostile boner. I'm probably safe at a Cubs game, but step one foot into a Father John Misty concert and I'll want to steer clear of the coffee sommelier wearing the Pendleton pashmina who's putting out grabby dance moves. And as for you, Betsy, if you believe this dangerous rhetoric that the system is set up against rapists, consider all the spaces you enter are rapist-friendly. Your bold eggplant suits might not rouse any violent chubs at Amoeba Music, but you might not be so safe at a Certified Public Accountants National Conference. No woman should have to put together an audit of all the places she'll be safe for every piece of clothing she wants to wear. Compare that amount of work and worry to being a dude walking the beach shirtless in Ibiza. Frat boys on EDM vacations are not worried someone is gonna sexually assault them.

The idea that clothing choices can stop men from raping is a frustratingly common belief having nothing to do with sexual assault. According to a study by A Federal Commission on Crime of Violence, rapists could not remember what their victims were wearing. So why do people continue to blame the clothing choices of women? Because it's *so hard* to teach men not to rape. If it were simple, you could go back to watching *The Steve Harvey*[9] *Show* and cross "safety of young women" off your worry list.[10] Association of American Universities conducted a couple of anonymous surveys to try getting to the bottom of why male students ignore consent. Here's what they found out:

1. MEN IGNORE CONSENT BECAUSE THEY'RE DRUNK.

In my personal opinion, alcohol is not an excuse; it's a magnifier. When I'm drunk, I Postmates a family-sized margherita pizza and will unapologetically eat the whole thing, and do you think I let a case of violent marinara and mozzarella vurps get in the way of showcasing my Sia dance skills to my husband and dog, who just want to go to sleep? No, because when I'm wasted, I'm committed to my art.

---

9   For a masterclass in victim blaming, check out Steve's advice. In an interview with Joy Behar, he explained that men cheat because "there are so many women out there willing to cheat with them."

10   I know what *is* on your worry list: "Is there a single college I'm welcome at?" and "Is Jesus TOO cute?"

2. MEN IGNORE CONSENT BECAUSE THEY FEEL PRESSURE TO HAVE SEX.

Guys are unable to apply the theory of "quality not quantity" to sexual experiences. A high number of sexual conquests has much more currency in the male world than spending months figuring out how to pleasure one woman. If dudes don't have the numbers to impress their shitty friends, they gotta juke the stats by adding in nonconsensual acts. This problem could be eradicated if guys followed my lead and responded to male pressure like this:

"Dude, you've only fucked three girls this year? Lame."

"Carlos, release yourself from the prison of masculinity and come back when you're chill, okay?"

3. MEN IGNORE CONSENT BECAUSE THEY BELIEVE THE MYTH THAT NO MEANS YES.

Let me tell you a true story about the wonders of Greek life. In 2014, the Texas Tech chapter of Phi Delta Theta had some horrific ideas for a hurricane-themed soiree they were throwing. I'll admit, I'm guilty of not knowing the first thing about throwing a natural disaster party. Does it involve begging State Farm to extend your flood insurance policy?

Rescuing a wheelchair-bound grandmother from a rooftop? Inviting only Katrinas, Sandys, and Irenes? Rum? I don't know. But Phi Delta Theta had some specific ideas about what would make this party the best tragedy rager TECH HAD EVER SEEN! And one of them was to hang banners printed with the message "No means Yes. Yes means Anal." They got the catchphrase from their fellow frat bros at Yale's Delta Kappa Epsilon, who made freshman pledges chant this in the quad, as some sort of hazing ritual to prove you have to be the worst if you want to be accepted by the worst.

Now, Betsy, I know we're not brain sisters. If we were, you'd be thinking what I'm thinking. Which is, when I'm on public transit and I hear someone loudly bragging about their involvement in Greek[11] life, I make a mental note that, should there be a crash or derailment, under NO CIRCUM-STANCES am I rescuing that person. Greek life is for people who lack the ability to meet friends in college, a place optimally designed to meet new people. It's redundant. The Greek system only makes sense if it was a way thirty-year-old R&D managers relocating from Philly to Denver could meet new friends.

---

11   I would, however, NEVER ignore an actual Greek person about to
        share a Thessaloniki hot tip on making the perfect taramasalata.

YOU WANT TO BE A DENVERITE?!
SIR, YES, SIR!
YOU WANT TO GO TO AN OLD CROW
MEDICINE SHOW AT RED ROCKS
WITH A BUNCH OF NEW FRIENDS
THIS WEEKEND?
SIR, YES, SIR!
THEN TAKE A SIP OF THIS SALMON
RIVER OATMEAL STOUT AND TELL
ME IF YOU THINK IT'S GOT TOO
MUCH BODY TO BE A PILSNER, YOU
LITTLE BITCH!

4. MEN IGNORE CONSENT BECAUSE THEY WATCH
RAPE PORN.

A young, curious man might stumble upon *Gang Rape of Wrath*, a sexy story where a bunch of well-hung Oklahoma tenant farmers bukakke Rose of Sharon while she breastfeeds a dying man. That same young male viewer might take away the wrong impression about the situation and forget he's watching *consenting* adults hump their way through John Steinbeck's haunting portrayal of the Great Depression.

5. MEN IGNORE CONSENT BECAUSE THEY'RE NARCISSISTS.

I'm so tired of narcissists. They ruin everything: America, healthy sexual interactions, all Los Angeles parties. Stand too long at the charcuterie plate and some dude named Todd will start droning on about the boring details of his backordered Tesla. Read your audience, Todd! I'm just here for the soppressata, not your lame personal struggle with a $74,000 fire hazard. I don't even know you!

All right, Betsy, hope you're feeling good about what you learned here. I'm sure you had to push out the memory of your first Bible camp or Kid Rock's phone number to make room for new information, and I thank you for your sacrifice. You now have the knowledge to make some important changes! Go out there, Secretary of Education—which, reminder, is your job—and EDUCATE dudes to not be rapists. Now, since I'm a thorough person, and I can tell you might be the kind of distracted lady who sits down to write your "No More Rape" manifesto but finds yourself on chicos.com looking for a braided spice market belt, I put together a plan for you.

No More Rape
By Betsy DeVos

Boys need to be taught what consent is by the PUBLIC school system starting in elementary school.[12] If a parent comes to the school and has a problem with their sons being taught to be nice people, have that parent arrested 'cause they're probably guilty of sexual assault. The learning should continue, through junior high and high school, with integrated sex ed lessons on what rape and sexual assault look like. They need to be taught why they might rape and why they might justify rape and why they shouldn't do any of those things. Then, by the time these educated men get to college, they know better than to say they'd grabbed a stranger's tits because they'd "lost their balance." And, if anyone slips through the cracks, they will be punished by the campus and the local police. Women will then be free to enjoy a life of safety and security.

The End.

---

12 If it were up to me, starting when they're born. They need to learn how to tap on their mommy's boobs and ask, "Dear mother, so sorry to trouble you, could I suckle your breast for my breakfast? Please and thank you."

Betsy, I've enjoyed our time together. Now, if I haven't persuaded you to protect women out of righteousness, allow me one final effort to get you to understand. You made millions of dollars on Amway, and my parents sold Amway for a month, so we basically speak the same language. Using the framework of a pyramid scheme (excuse me, "multi-level marketing opportunity"), think about it this way—we want every guy to reach Founders Crown Ambassador level nonrapist, but they're not even at Silver Producer nonrapist, so we need to give them incentives. The fewer women they rape, the closer they get to climbing the levels AND, while they're racking up points not raping, they can recruit guys to work under them to also not rape. And then those guys can recruit nonrape distributors and so on and so on until their downline (multi-leveler insider term) is earning them so much nonassault they are soaring through the levels! Think of the possibilities! If we can recruit this many nonrapists, we could revolutionize the way men treat women! Success is just a decision away! Every man becomes a nonraper by choice! So, Betsy, let's go out there and show Herbalife who's better at selling no rape!!!!

LESBIANS ARE NONE OF OUR BUSINESS

I am not a member of the LGBTQ community. I'm just a straight ally who, on behalf of my cis-gendered heterosexuals, would like to apologize. A lot of us are unable to let you live your lives the way you choose because we are so concerned with what you can do for us. Will you watch us suck off a banana and tell us how we can improve our BJ technique? Will you be joining us at Trina Turk to give us guttural reactions to Moroccan-inspired jumpsuits? Will you be answering our texts about whether or not our face is too old to bleach and tone our hair platinum white (sorry, Trixie Mattel and Jonathan Van Ness)? Will you be cooking us a crispy, oven-roasted chicken while listening to us drone on about why we can't get the guy who hates us to love us? And oh my God, did we drink all the sparkling rosé already? Could you be a doll and run out for some more? YOU'RE THE BEST I LOVE YOU THANKKKKKSSSS!

Straight-ees love us a gaggle of helper homos, and we're so self-obsessed we're even taking credit for their sexual identities. To understand this phenomenon, let's take a trip to the University of Nicosia in Cyprus—a sweet little republic right by Greece and Turkey. Menelaos Apostolou (rolls right off the tongue, right?) is an associate professor of evolutionary psychology who has dedicated his life to studying modern behavior through the lens of evolution. He's big in the field. I know you've seen his work like "Parental Mate Choice Manipulation Tactics" or "A Cross-Cultural Investigation of the Evolutionary Origins of Athletic Behavior." Ring any bells? Was made into a HUGE movie. Remember the poster? Ben Affleck dressed as an anthropologist holding a magnifying glass up to a bicep.

My point is, Ben Affleck's career choices are hit and miss AND Menelaos is a big deal in his field. Being an evolution cuck, he's trying to understand the biological basis of human behavior. For example, regarding lesbians, why would women have sex with other women unless there was something in it for straight dudes?

For his scientific study, Menelaos surveyed the EXPERTS on homosexual behavior—1,509 heterosexuals—and discovered that lesbianism is not a natural sexual inclination. In fact, according to this study, it's an evolutionary adaptive behavior women developed over time when they realized their kissing made straight men horny. You might recall the famous line from Sappho's poem "Ode to Aphrodite" where she muses:

Aphrodite, how I long to kiss your lips.
To caress your breast.
All so that Odysseus might jerk off onto his leg.

About half of the men in Menelaos's study reported they would become sexually excited if their opposite-sex partners revealed to them that they experienced same-sex attraction.

Guys would like to see two women make out? Okay. Here's some other stuff I've known my whole life—dill pickles taste good on sandwiches and my mom is legally obligated to stay in Marshalls for at least four hours. But brushing aside the obvious revelations about straight male libido, the conclusion reached by Cyprus's premier behaviorist porn scientist is bass-ackwards. Concluding lesbians kiss to give straight men boners is like saying pollock commit suicide so

McDonald's can make Filet-O-Fish, a meal I absolutely eat.[1]

The women surveyed did not have the same reaction—only 7.8 percent of them said they would be turned on if their male partner kissed a man. They'd better be glad I wasn't part of this study.

"Would you be turned on if your partner kissed a man?"

"No."

"Would you be turned on if your partner kissed a woman?"

"No."

"Would you be turned on if you came home and your partner was organizing your shirt closet by color, subdivided by sleeve length?"

"OH GOD! I'M CREAMING MY SKORTS!!!! GET A BUCKET!!!"[2]

It's worth pointing out that Menelaos's own data doesn't support his theory. If straight women aren't interested in watching two guys named Mark in

---

1   If you think I stopped after Trump said he loved it, you are dead wrong, sister. Nothing can stop me from wrapping my wine-dehydrated lips around that stale bun, pasteurized American cheese, almost rotten tartar sauce, and square fish Frankenstein.

2   And here's why: (1) My husband does not organize like this and (2) we'll never have enough money to have a house with so many closets we can dedicate one to just his shirts. The aspirational order and storage space makes me hot in my bottom.

neon green mesh tanks take turns dipping their dicks in each other's mouths, then maybe, um, homosexuals don't have sex to please us. What's more likely is the guys in this study are constantly sexcited and would probably get a boner if a Mediterranean breeze tickled their linen shorts the right way.

Menelaos is not the only straight guy who can't wrap his mind around women doing something pleasurable for themselves only. Return of the Kings— an aggro male jizz heap of a website, read by millions of garbage people—once published a piece called "How to Seduce a Lesbian as a Straight Man." Much like gastroenteritis, it quickly went viral. Thank you, thank you, you can see me every Friday at Grossinger's in the Catskills. It's abandoned, so just follow the lone flashlight coming from the graffitied diving board. We'll have a bunch of LOLs.

The piece was written by Eric Crowley, an understanding man who spends his time writing charming, cocktail party fare like "American Children Are the Prisoners of Women," "8 Reasons to Date a Former Fat Girl," and "Can Female Circumcision Prevent Throat Cancer in Men?"[3] Crowley is THE expert

---

3   He's clearly angry about male circumcision and instead of advocating that it be stopped, wants women to suffer the same mutilation. Or maybe he's the world's worst satirist, but he's still angry and likes to write about female mutilation. I happen to agree with his main point. I think male circumcision is a TRAVESTY and Amer-

on how to seduce lesbians because he's actually done it. "I've had sex with a full-on gold-star lesbian, and made out with several more," he writes. That's not special, Eric. You've just described every night at a Ruby Rose DJ set.

The first thing Eric does in his piece is convince guys why they'd even want to bother to seduce a lesbian. I would assume anyone landing on his blog post had already made up their mind, but it never hurts to be double triple sure when challenging someone's sexual preference, Billy Graham style. He writes:

Lesbians combine the fantasy of hot girl-on-girl action, with a woman who is untouched by other men. Someone who is deeply sexual, experienced, and a "virgin" at the same time.

Here's a secret most straight guys don't know— no adult woman is ever a virgin. We all lose our virginity to spa jets at a very young age. When I see a

---

ica's obsession with angular shiny genitals is depriving men from the Atlantic to the Pacific of powerful, neighbor-bothering orgasms. Eric could do a lot of good if he wasn't walking toe fungus zipped up in golfer's skin, strutting around town showing off his invisible lats in a large-print polo shirt and spreading his toxic hate. Or maybe he's a pile of gnats feasting on donkey shit who prefers muted wrinkle-resistant gray brown button-downs and his rimless glasses as he eats tuna out of a can while he adds hateful rhetoric to the Internet's awful bank. I have to guess what he looks like because he's not brave enough to put his picture on the Internet.

Jacuzzi, I think, "There it is, the one that got away." The classic "show me the blood on the sheets" definition of virginity is tired and played out. If you've had a finger, fist, or vibrator attached to a refrigerator (like I saw a lady do on *Real Sex*) in your vagina, you're not a virgin. Keep doing you and bypass all the troglodytes who stick to the "dicks only" definition.

Because Crowley really gets lesbians (i.e., accidentally heard a Melissa Etheridge song once while grocery shopping at Ralphs), he knows all the things straight guys do wrong when trying to seduce them:

> Guys will try to tell these women they just haven't found the right man yet, or that all she needs is some good "deep dicking."

Crowley goes on to bro-splain that this is a terrible thing to say to a lesbian, but before you give him credit for having a rice grain of humanity, let me tell you *why* he says it's not cool. It's not because telling a lesbian she needs corrective sex with a penis is a horrific conversation starter, but because it's "bad game." He thinks dudes shouldn't tell a lesbian she needs a deep dicking because it's ineffective flirting. A better way to approach a lesbian is to "take her sexual orientation as a disqualifier, rather than rejection. Playfully tease her about it. Tell her all the reasons you could never be together, because of *your* standards, not hers."

This is called "negging," the art of being a stupid troll in the hope someone has been so deprived of love their whole life they're willing to give you a chance. The goal being to insult flirt until you fuck the girl and then run away like a rat in the night. Then you're off to insult the next fuck hole and on and on until your dick is so raw from fucking so many sluts you have to swat away the skanks so your cock doesn't fall off. Those are my words, reinterpreting their words, to illustrate their intent.

Crowley advises isolating the lesbian target so her friends don't see her abandoning her sexual identity for a fuckable Internet stud. But if you look deep into Crowley's piece, he's accidentally giving us real information about why straight guys are so obsessed with figuring out why lesbians aren't into them. He says:

> It's no secret that many lesbians aren't lesbians because they like women, but because they hate men.

Let's breeze past how insulting it is to write off a sexual orientation as a last resort. He's saying—subconsciously—it would be easier for straight guys to accept lesbians if they thought the only reason women were lesbians is because they hate men. But that's not why women are lesbians. Women are lesbians because they like cats. I'm sorry, I meant "pussy." Straight guys aren't even in the equation, aren't even considered, which is hard for these dudes to deal with.

According to his Twitter, Crowley has retired from "manosphere" writing,[4] but his Internet words live on forever and the beliefs he subscribes to about lesbians continue to permeate the culture. According to a 2015 OFFICIAL AS FUCK report from Pornhub, which broke down most popular searches by topic, the number one porn search term in the United States is "lesbian." It's a fantasy being reinforced by easy access to millions of hours of straight ladies fingering each other in pink marbled bathtubs. Straight guys aren't interested in actual lesbian porn, where a Lea DeLaria butch dyke passionately eats out some lezboi in nothing but a Cross Colours hat.

The loads of woman-on-woman porn is making

---

4   How not shocked would you be if you found out that this Eric Crowley guy was now working under Jeff Sessions? "I don't know, one day I was writing shitty things on the Internet about women and the next day I had a highly classified job at the attorney general's office."

****   By the way, side note of all side notes—did you know Jeff Sessions's middle name is Beauregard? Jeffrey Beauregard Sessions III. His parents were like, "We need a name that will leave no question about his devotion to the purity of the white race. Like Foghorn Leghorn...but classy."

life harder for lesbians, but it's not the only tech-
nological problem they face. People are also using
Tinder, the fuck app, to match with other women
only to reveal that they're actually looking to match
them with their vagina AND their boyfriend's dick.
I'd be pissed if I matched with a dude I liked/wanted
to bone on Tinder, before finding out the price for
entry was eating out his girlfriend (better than he
could). No thanks. I have to assume a lesbian getting
a message from a sexy lady might experience the
same disappointment when she finds out there's a
dick toll to access pussy bridge.[5]

In America, it might seem fun for guys to approach a lesbian with the angle of hooking up.
Harmless even. It can *seem* that way, but it is often
much more loaded. It thrives on thinking that a
woman who does not desire men needs to be chal-
lenged or fixed. Lesbians don't need to be fixed; they
need to be left alone to seek pleasure and com-
panionship with each other, start families, and build
impressive patios.

So, if you know this dude, the kind of man who
fantasizes about two women making out, tell him he
doesn't get to go up to Kristen Stewart when she's
chain-smoking outside of the Delta terminal and try

---

5   Please, if you take anything away from this book, I hope it's this
    analogy.

to convince her to fuck him. Tell him if a lesbian wants to fuck him (she doesn't), let her come to him (she won't). Until then, he should do everyone a favor and stick to "lesbian" porn and keep his unsolicited desires in his three-dollar boxer briefs.

STAYING OUT OF MAY/DECEMBER ROMANCES

As he pulled his long, withered dick out of Shanna's supple female parts, William Holmquist Spreckles IV coated her young, voluptuous bush with a dusty plume of ghost sperm. "Don't throw up, don't throw up," she told herself, running her youthful hands through his Crypt Keeper hair wisps. Shanna's eyes fixated on William's dark, merlot-colored liver spots, sun damage she pretended were root beer jelly beans. "Tell me you love me, tell me I'm the only man you want to be with," William begged, his antiquated vocal cords struggling to sustain the sentence. "Yeah, sure, okay," she lied, trying to avoid the sight of his white, wiry pubic hair. Satisfied with the answer

and imbued with the last gasp of his morning
Viagra, he traced the outline of her nipples with
his Skeletor fingers. "You complete me," he
said. "That's from *Jerry Maguire*." "What's that?"
Shanna asked. "It was a movie from before you
were born."

—An excerpt from the romance novel *The
Beautiful Mistress and the Man Who Knew
Calvin Coolidge*

It's a classic story: Some woman, in the "May" of her
life, suddenly appears in a "December" man's world,
and injects his old, sad soul with the vitality and joy
he was unable to find in a woman his own age. December women are crusty-skinned shrews who have
the audacity to complain about lower back pain. May
women don't have back problems! They can do im-
promptu backflips on the Santa Monica pier[1] while
holding their Pomeranian named Snapchat. May
women are dewy-skinned adherents of the mystical
YOLO philosophy with perky boobs and whimsical
drink orders. "Bubble gum vodka, Sprite, and a Blow
Pop, please. Oh, and can you serve it to me in a
stemless wineglass etched with a cat dressed like a

---

1 Can you believe she even agreed to go to the Santa Monica pier!?
A December woman would have complained about the hell trip
that place is, with the two hours of traffic, impossible parking, rude
tourists, and overpriced corn dogs wafting over the dead fish smell.

lawyer? Thannnnnks!" May women don't understand checks or *Cheers* references and your dad likes it that way.[2]

I am the direct result of a May vagina and a December dick. My mom was a hot, sixteen-year-old May; my dad a charismatic midthirties December who'd opened a photography studio in small-town Ohio. Do you want to see photos my dad took of my mom topless with a boa while she was still in high school? Me neither, but I've seen them. It was the beginning of their love affair and it ended with my mom's pregnancy. But they did the "right" thing and spent twenty years of their lives raising me and my sister, trying very hard to make their relationship seem "normal."

The May/December relationship was the example I was raised with, and so it should shock no one that I tried to fuck a teacher when I was a senior in high school. He was twenty-five; I was seventeen. For the sake of anonymity, let's call him Buddy Holly, a shy man, tall with an athletic build, adorable crooked smile, and calm presence, fresh out of college and now living in a boring suburb. I'd had a crush on him for about a year, so when I found out he had an

---

2 I'm not saying there aren't rare exceptions of a woman falling madly in love with an older man for pure reasons like they both love rescuing ferrets or met at a group for Satanists or something niche like that. If you're one of those exceptions, mazel tov!

open spot for a teacher's assistant, I snatched it up and proceeded to dump buckets of adoration on him. I did everything in my power to get him to make a move on me: wearing see-through tops, grazing his leg with mine, giving him sketches of tattoos I was thinking about getting (not a joke). But Buddy Holly had too much integrity.

One day, we were alone while I was helping him in the equipment room. I stood under the soccer ball shelf and as he reached above me, he was so close I could feel his arm's peach fuzz brushing against my shoulder. We stared at each other like two hungry jackals. I pictured the next moment in my head: It was just as plausible to imagine us fucking in the equipment room as it was to imagine us continuing to stand there awkwardly. It ended up as the latter.

Once I found out where he lived, I would jog past on Saturdays wearing a teeny sports bra and cameltoe-y Spandex shorts to wave hello as he pulled weeds in his front yard. The consequences of what I was doing were not clear to me. Relationships were a new thing for me, so I was stumbling around like a toddler barreling toward the sharp corners of a glass coffee table. Despite my "fuck me, please fuck me" campaign, nothing lurid ever transpired between us. In the history of humankind, no young woman has ever worked harder to get an adult to sleep with her than I did that year. When I graduated, the infinite flirtation ended. But it kicked off my nearly perfect record of dating older men: my best friend's older brother; the corporate lawyer I met as an intern in college; an ex-marine who sold Aflac, owned a handgun, and listened to Rusted Root. Aflac said before he met me, he thought his dick was broken. Up until that point, it was the most romantic thing anyone had ever said to me. The patterns I repeated reinforced my worldview—I was too mature for guys my age and by dating older men, not only did I have the company of people on my level, I could learn things guys my age didn't know. Did I like chianti? What *was* supplemental insurance? How many types of French cheeses are good in omelets?[3] Important life stuff twenty-year-old dudes didn't know. Living in Chicago after college, I dated a guy who was exactly my age until he punched me in the arm at a Pixies concert. He was shocked I didn't know "Bone Machine" and so he hit me like I was his bro. Of course I didn't know "Bone Machine"! How could I know all the Pixies' songs when I was busy listening to Chicago's "You're the Inspiration" in the Porsche of a thirty-eight-year-old British accountant?!

---

3   One—Boursin pepper cheese.

Less than a year after the Pixies punch, when I was twenty-five, I married my first husband, who was in his early thirties, seven weeks after we met. One night, we were naked, wrapped in blankets, and he floated a theory that we both needed each other to heal from our aloof parents. But then I went to therapy for five years and figured out I could fix myself, which allowed me to reevaluate how I felt about my marriage. After six years, I decided I *didn't* like being woken up at 2:00 a.m. to talk him down off some hypothetical disaster ledge he had climbed onto, there were *other* gifts I would like to get on our anniversary outside of Israeli gas masks, and my feelings *did* get hurt every year when he couldn't remember my birthday (or be bothered to write it down) but did know his ever-changing PlayStation password. So, on Christmas Day, I celebrated the birth of baby Jesus by asking my husband for a divorce.[4]

What these May/December relationships ended up doing was delaying my ability to grow. I didn't know what it was like to have a sexual experience with another person who was equally as curious and dumb. I didn't know what it was like to learn *with*

---

4 We're still great friends and I love his new wife, who is so patient and kind. I'm happy she inherited all the work I put in changing him via my emotional outbursts.

someone else. I didn't know for a long time that most of the men in Texas were not for me. I was too busy being taught what "matters" in life by men five to ten years older, who saw Pearl Jam when they were just an opening act.

Woody Allen—a scrawny, dead-eyed avatar for Jewish male neurosis—fully encapsulates this ethos. There's a fucking disturbing 2016 interview in the *Hollywood Reporter* with Woody Allen[5] in which he reflects upon all the ways he helped his wife (and stepdaughter), Soon-Yi. Try and get through this without throwing up your turkey club:

> She had a very, very difficult upbringing in Korea: She was an orphan on the streets, living out of trash cans and starving as a 6-year-old. And she was picked up and put in an orphanage. And so I've been able to really make her life better. I provided her with enormous opportunities, and she has sparked to them...So the

---

5 I believe Dylan Farrow's accusations even more after reading these interviews. After the *Washington Post*'s Richard Morgan went through Allen's personal notes at Princeton University and concluded the writer-director is obsessed with teenage girls, I believe her even more more more more more. Woody Allen seems like a man hell-bent on teaching women how to please him, whether by his art or by other means. I draw a very clear line in the sand when it comes to separating artists from their art. I do not support with my time or money people who I believe to be enemy of women. Your turn, Blake Lively, Diane Keaton, and Kate Winslet.

contributions I've made to her life have given me more pleasure than all my films.

Not gross enough for you? How about this 2015 interview with *Paper* magazine:

I'm 35 years older, and somehow, through no fault of mine or hers, the dynamic worked. I was paternal. She responded to someone paternal. I liked her youth and energy. She deferred to me, and I was happy to give her an enormous amount of decision making just as a gift and let her take charge of so many things.

Jesus take the wheel. "I liked her youth and energy" is something a fantasy villain says before using an amulet to suck the life force out of a newborn. "Now youth and energy shall be MINE!" Good thing Woody Allen came into her life to save her, otherwise Soon-Yi would have been stuck going to pig wrastlin' 'n' participatin' in hot dog eating contests with her mom, Mia Farrow. I mean, just look at Ronan. Guy can barely walk out of the house with a clean shirt on and I'm not even sure he can read. I heard he has to carry a dictionary with him to look up words at Dunkin' Donuts.

Woody Allen is the perfect December man, and because he's naturally unable to stop words from escaping his mouth, he can give us an accurate look inside the mind of a perv without showing an ounce of self-reflection. Why else use the phrase "somehow the dynamic worked"? He knows it worked because he's a smart guy. He followed the formula—convince a young girl she desperately needs you as a papa figure because she's not yet confident she can take care of herself.

The idea that younger women are more mature than men their age is a falsehood serving men well. When some old lecherous man sexualizes us before we have our learner's permit, he can justify his behavior with this widely accepted lie.

That said, according to fivethirtyeight.com, my intergenerational romances were far from "normal." Turns out the average age difference among couples is 2.3 years. That's nothing! And the 2013 census found only 4.8 percent of hetero married couples had a wifey more than ten years younger. So what the fuck? Why does it feel like a whole generation of nubile twentysomethings are doting on silver foxes? Maybe it's because the old boners running Hollywood are cranking out May/December romances like their lives depended on it. Have you ever seen Helen Mirren kiss Michael Douglas, a man her exact age? No, 'cause Hollywood wants you to see Michael Douglas kiss Rachel McAdams while she's teaching him how to Dougie.

Kyle Buchanan at Vulture took a FRIGHTEN-
ING look at leading men versus the age of their love
interests. What you're seeing in every Denzel
Washington/Tom Cruise/George Clooney/Liam
Neeson/Johnny Depp/Richard Gere film is movie
magic—these leading men keep getting older while
their love interests stay around the same ages.[6] Olivia
Wilde at twenty-nine played the love interests of both
Steve Carell, who was fifty at the time they starred in
The Incredible Burt Wonderstone, and Liam Neeson, who
was sixty-one in *The Third Person*. Maggie Gyllenhaal
lost an acting job because she was told that, at thirty-
seven, she was simply too old to play the love interest
of a fifty-five-year-old. You know what Maggie
Gyllenhaal is too old for? Playing a seven-year-old
Marie Curie. She is not too old for a *fifty-five-year-old
man* to find her attractive! Turning someone down for
a job based on their age is called discrimination. But
pre-#MeToo Hollywood was largely able to convince the public (and itself) that it's liberal and progressive while secretly acting like the worst conservatives when it came to respecting women.

---

6   The Wooderson effect. Made famous in my mind thanks to the
    Matthew McConaughey character in *Dazed and Confused* who
    opines, "That's what I like about high school girls, I get older, they
    stay the same age." I'd like to think when I first saw the movie at fif-
    teen that I thought, "What a predator," but I probably thought, "I
    hope a guy like that falls in love with me one day!"

And that's not the most disgusting thing you'll read in the next five minutes. Stephen Follows at IndieWire did his own number crunching to look into the age-gap issues in films and uncovered a real turd of an example—1984's *Blame It on Rio*. Listen to this vurp of a movie plot: Michael Caine is on vacation in Rio de Janeiro with his best friend and their daughters, and the twist is, he starts fucking his best friend's daughter. She was eighteen in the movie and in real life; Caine was fifty-one! Can you imagine leaving a Dua Lipa show before hearing "New Rules" so you can go to your dad's friend's condo to climb on his dick before 9:00 p.m. because he has a morning flight to run a property management conference in Phoenix? I fell in love with a twenty-five-year-old when I was seventeen and even I thought he was old. No teenage girl wants to fuck a fifty-one-year-old man! She wants to fuck a dumb, ripped quarterback who whispers sweet nothings in her ear like, "Be a dude and hand me my beer koozie." *Blame It on Rio* is based on the French film *Un moment d'égarement* because of course it is. Here are the fucking French[7] again,

---

7   French PM Emmanuel Macron is married to a woman twenty-five years older. She was his drama teacher and they fell in love when he was fifteen, and I would like to say this is not a great example of settling the score. Fifteen-year-old boys are gross, even French ones, even French ones played by Timothée Chalamet.

doing their "charming" pervert thing. They are a country who heard Serge Gainsbourg's *Histoire de Melody Nelson* and cried "*Oui, oui,* more songs about a grown man seducing a fifteen-year-old." In the trailer for *Blame It on Rio*, Michael Caine, as "Dad the Statutory Rapist," justifies the affair by saying, "You're never too old to be crazy."[8] Yes, you are. But Roger Ebert, in his review of the film, took a different perspective:

It's really unsettling to see how casually this movie takes a serious situation. A disturbed girl is using sex to play mind games with a middle-aged man.

Whoa, whoa, whoa, deceased film critic. It's *her* fault, Roger Ebert? The actress who plays the love interest was seventeen when they began shooting and had to get THE PERMISSION OF A JUDGE to film the nude scenes. It hardly speaks well of a minor's power if she's not even allowed to make her own decisions about her nude scene. Men, critics, and actors need to start speaking up when they sign

---

8   The director of *Blame It on Rio* also directed *Singin' in the Rain.* Actually kind of makes sense. Gene Kelly was thirty-nine and Debbie Reynolds nineteen. In Reynolds's memoir *Unsinkable* she said Gene "shoved his tongue down my throat." She freaked and asked for a Coke to rinse her mouth out.

their deals, including in their riders, a clause stating they won't star opposite women more than five years their junior. Eradicating the media's glorification of the May/December romance AND giving older working actresses more opportunities? Sounds like a very groundbreaking one-two punch. Right, George Clooney? In 2012, he told *EW*:

> When a man hits 40 is when roles just begin to happen. And for women it doesn't happen. I find that to be a very concerning issue.

So, as one of the highest-grossing leading men of all time, why don't you do something about it? When you, the moviegoer, see a movie poster where the love interests look like father and daughter, skip it. Grab yourself a couple of limes and some tequila, and watch as Nancy Meyers makes two age-appropriate people with impossibly white kitchens fall in love with each other.

All of this, in my opinion, is the death rattle of coverture. William Blackstone, in his eighteenth-century treatise *Commentaries of the Law of England*, explained the law this way:

> The very being or legal existence of the woman is suspended during the marriage, or at least is incorporated and consolidated into that of

the husband: under whose wing, protection, and cover, she performs everything;

This idea is still clinging to women—women who think they can only gain protection and care from men who are able to provide for them. And what safer bet than an older, well-established man? We have freed ourselves from the legal idea that we're the property of men, so let's stop thinking we need something from them. Remove that factor and be with someone because they make you happy. Because they respect you. Because they treat you like an equal.

There will always be guys like Hugh Hefner, wiping off his 1950s baby-oiled dick so he can army crawl over to the next barely legal plaything fingering herself on his satin sheets. You don't need them. Pose in *Playboy* if you want but take the money and buy some real estate and start being your own well of support.

When I was thirty years old, I was divorced from my older husband and very lost. It was the fire I needed to fix myself. I built up my savings, dedicated myself to yoga and therapy—cried in both—and worked on being happy by myself. When I met my second husband at a party, I didn't need a thing from him. Just his presence. You don't need an older man to show you the world, to teach you about good food, to help you. You just need yourself.

LET THE TEENS FUCK EACH OTHER

Colleen Merckbox stands stoically in front of the classroom. Draped head to toe in dramatically distressed denim, she holds a beautiful rose in front of her face. The fluorescent lights reflect off her brassy highlights as her weighty mascara fights with her violet-painted eyelids. She's beautiful…in an '80s, New Orleans rodeo clown kind of way. Colleen hands the rose to a circle of Jefferson High's finest young women. "Each of y'all take one petal, then pass it round," Colleen barks. The women do as instructed as Colleen half sits on a desk, psychotically twitching her right leg. One by one the students mutilate the blossom. When the last petal is removed, Colleen snatches the bare, thorny stem. "See what happens when you give your sex petals away, ladies?" she says. "You go from a beautiful virgin flower to a thorny useless slut stem. Don't be a flower whore, got it?"

Meet America's abstinence educators. Colleen is fictional, but she's just like the real ones: dumb, mean, and possessed by a strange affinity for dramatic props. While they throw their scary stats and misogynist nonsense at the entire student body, they reserve most of their ire and shame for all the young lady sluts in the bleachers.

To understand how these psychologically maladjusted adults came to infiltrate our nation's schools, let's take a trip back to the early 2000s. The president, George W. Bush, wasn't the laid-back Renaissance painter everyone knows and loves today. He was (is) a warmonger and the king of a ruined U.S. economy. But that wasn't enough chaos for Mr. Mission Accomplished. Just for funsies, he ushered in a new era of abstinence-only education. Under his presidency, we got Title XI, Section 1110 of the Social Security Act, which gave federal money to community and faith-based organizations to teach abstinence-only education and leave out any important information about safe sex or contraception. So, federally funded deception.

Since its inception, over $2 BILLION has been spent in this country trying to talk teens out of the funnest activity Jesus ever invented. There's no data on how many abstinence educators suddenly became qualified to teach these federally funded courses, but there seems to be a lot of them. Enough to not just incorrectly screw in a lightbulb, but also shoot our nation's lightbulbs to pieces, plunging our country into eternal darkness. And they're all variations of the same confusing combination of women's prison guard, your blowhard divorced uncle, and a Parisian balloon animal artist. Let's meet some of them.

Pam Stenzel arrives at public schools in her funky jean jacket and Elvis-like swagger, ready to fight evil female sexuality. According to her website—which she wrote in 8-point font because she has A LOT TO SAY and we all know websites have finite space— Pam got her start working in "pregnancy crisis centers," the Venus flytrap of women's organizations. Women think they're going in for medically accredited abortion help, but what they too often get is a bunch of pro-life propagandists armed with an ultrasound machine and misleading stats to scare them out of abortions. It's medical coercion by antichoice thugs and the perfect training ground for an abstinence educator.

Instead of shaming one woman at a time, Pam can now guilt hundreds in a single afternoon. She likes to stand on a high school auditorium stage (hopefully with the set of the senior production of *Little Shop of Horrors* still up) and scare lots of young women about sex leading to scarred fallopian tubes. I suppose she's going buck wild with all the potential horrors of untreated sexually transmitted diseases, but I prefer to believe Pam thinks some sort of deformed sharp penis could corkscrew its way through the vagina, into the uterus, and then up into the fallopian tubes. Not surprisingly, in order for her program to be eligible for money, it only has to meet eight guidelines under another abstinence grant system, Title V of the Welfare Reform Act, and none of them dictate her to include medically accurate information. If it did, Pam couldn't pad her lectures with tidbits about how abortion can lead to anorexia, bulimia, and cutting[1]—which she might have pulled from a 2009 study by Priscilla Coleman and her colleagues at Bowling Green University finding that abortions can lead to future mental health issues. A study that was discredited by University of California's Julia Steinberg and the Guttmacher Institute's Lawrence Finer because, DUMB BITCH ALERT, Priscilla didn't take into account if those women had mental health issues *before* their abortions. I'm not a boxing fan, but I would buy front-row tickets to watch Julia Steinberg eviscerate Priscilla Coleman

---

1 Scaring women out of abortions by saying they could end up with an eating disorder, as if it's some sort of punishment. Super shitty to say that in front of a group of women likely to be struggling with eating disorders. Pam's out to prove she don't know nuthin' about nuthin' and never will.

with knowledge. But like with drag queen rules, so they'd say stuff like, "Priscilla, your data collection's so sloppy, cafeterias be serving them between two buns and calling it lunch. Okuuurt!"

The luxury Pam has as an abstinence educator is she doesn't really need to fact-check. She can put on her denim bathrobe, pop open her industrial-sized laptop, pull whatever official-sounding word bites off the Internet, and still have time to watch her favorite episodes of *Last Man Standing*, which, yeah, she owns on DVD. She probably doesn't even have to search for all her "facts" since I am guessing she can just make them up. According to the *Charleston Gazette-Mail*, in 2013 a student at a West Virginia high school reported that Pam had told her classmates that if they take birth control, their mom probably hates them.

Okay, Pam, what if these ladies, like me, let their significant other pull out and shoot his meat creme all over their back? Where does that fall on this twisted scale? And her advice to boys is simple—if you see a girl "dressing in that manner—and you know what I'm talking about—that says to you and every other boy in the county 'take me now,' a little word of advice boys, *Run*!"[2]

Have you ever wondered what kind of person

---

2 Pam's lessons are available in eleven different languages if you're curious how to slut-shame in Mandarin.

could be magic-spelled into existence if a witch threw a Diet Mr. Pibb, a Spanish-teacher haircut, an S&M-adjacent statement belt, and a mauve fringe jacket into a cauldron? Wonder no longer! Presenting abstinence super-educator Shelly Donahue. Shelly is part of an abstinence-until-marriage organization called WAIT (Why Am I Tempted), which has gobbled up over $8.2 million in federal funds[3] to make young women feel like trash in public schools, churches, and community centers throughout Colorado. There's a lot of money in abstinence education, and they invest $1 to $2 packing their sex-shaming presentations with terrible props.[4] Shelly's known in the abstinence world for her amazing tape demonstration that really drives home to men why they shouldn't risk putting their innocent cherub dicks into nasty young women. She has a male volunteer pretend a piece of tape is his new girlfriend and excitedly delivers the joke, "Look, she's very transparent!" before instructing him to expose his "naked" forearm so he and the tape can "have sex" in front of everyone. Shelly then sticks the tape to his

---

3   I didn't know slut-shaming was so expensive; on *The Bachelor* they make it look free.
4   And explosive visuals. She calls premarital sex "squirt gun sex" and marital sex "fireworks sex." As someone who has fucked in and out of marriages, I can assure the women, it's always gonna be squirt gun sex. Just don't let him squirt gun you in the eyes. It burns.

forearm and exclaims, "Look! They've bonded," like she's a scientist who just discovered the concept of adhesive. She then cruelly makes the boy break up with his cellophane "girlfriend," a process similar to a bikini wax but with less excruciating labial stinging. Using the overdramatic hand gestures of a low-rent David Blaine, she points at the now gnarled tape. "Look at his little hairs," she says. "Look at his skin cells and his DNA, and his lotion and his cologne, and his germs and his sweat." Shelly brings up another volunteer and asks him to "get naked on his arm." She tries to stick the tape on but—shocker—it's less sticky. Shelly's fringe jacket jingles as she uses her acrylic nails to gesture to the grizzled piece of tramp tape. She then drives her point home—"How many partners do we have before we get married on average in America?" She cringes. "Six, yeah. So can you imagine what's going to start to happen to the tape? It's gonna lose its bonding power."

Because Shelly is so unwilling to do any hard research to back up her claims, she doesn't know the average number of premarital sexual partners is actually higher! Think of all the sluts she could scare with real facts! According to a 2015 study by San Diego State University psych professor Jean Twenge, the Greatest Generation averaged three sexual partners in their lifetime; Boomers nearly quadrupled that number to eleven, and Gen X and Millennials reported having had ten and eight sexual partners, respectively. I've had twenty-four sexual partners. I know the exact number because I keep a spreadsheet named "Guys I've had sex with" and that is the truth. It's in my Google drive. They're all in there—the Pauls and Michaels and some whose names I don't remember so they're listed as Karate Guy and Rachel's Friend with the '80s Steve Jobs Glasses. According to Shelly's logic, my pussy tape should be so loose I could effortlessly slide a Simplehuman dual-compartment waste bin inside me. But joke's on her. I'm tighter than Sarah Huckabee Sanders's stress-clenched butthole on a Friday afternoon.

Not to be outdone in the bold look department is abstinence educator Justin "Call Me By My Real Name" Lookadoo, who's putting his own spin on frosted tips, Ed Hardy knockoff button-downs, and distressed jeans. His look says to the world, "Yes, I *am* the Vanilla Ice of Hootie & the Blowfish." Justin wrote a book for teens with the razzle-dazzle title *Dateable: Are You? Are They?*, which teaches women that the best way to get to know the man they're dating is to zip their pie holes. He writes:

Be mysterious. Dateable girls know how to shut up. They don't monopolize the conversation. They don't tell everyone everything about themselves. They save some for later. They listen more than they gab.

Silence is not mysterious. You know what's mysterious? Wearing a vampire cloak at all times. Suddenly speaking fluent Flemish. Leaving a restaurant via grappling hook. That's creating mystery! Anyone who wants to go on a date with a mute woman is an incurious narcissist who just wants to fuck you while they look at themselves in their sliding closet mirror—which, I'm here to tell you, is distracting.

Justin uses a lot of literary tricks in his book, like poetically referring to women as prey to be hunted by men, fish taking bait, and uncharted territory to be conquered. If you told me his apartment was stacked floor to ceiling with Gothic gold titled medieval fantasy paperbacks wilted in a way indicating years of jizz-covered hand holding, my level of shock would be "nonexistent."

When Lookadoo's not teaching young girls how to be docile prey in his "advice" books, he's lecturing IRL teen girls about how dumb they are. At Richardson High School in Richardson, Texas, senior Aisleen Menezes wrote a blog about Justin's speech that went viral. In her telling, Lookadoo told the auditorium, "Ladies, I'm going to say this in the nicest way possible…you are the most horrible, awful, vindictive creatures this planet has ever seen."

What the fuck does women shutting up or being vindictive have to do with not having sex? Nothing. I guess abstinence education is one of the most lucrative career paths for people who hate women.[5] And why do they all dress so terribly? Is it part of the abstinence education uniform to suffocate all sexuality with denim?

Justin Lookadoo is allowed to harbor whatever long-standing grudge he probably has against some woman for a toothy blowjob he got in 1996. Pam Stenzel should be free to stew about her fifteen-year-old mother giving her up for adoption or whatever chip she has on her shoulder about women and their sexuality. They're all allowed to hate women. But what they're not allowed to do is drown themselves in so much chambray while also taking their irrational emotions out on young women desperate for answers about their sexual health and well-being.

We didn't have abstinence education at Cypress Falls High School, but we did have Young Life, an after-school Christian program that, according to

---

5 Outside of the entertainment industry. I'm very grateful that I grew up with the militant morally hypocritical in Texas. It's the only thing that prepared me to deal with the utter dysfunction of Hollywood. During one of my first meetings in LA, a producer, who happened to be Meghan Markle's ex-husband, made fun of my shoes. Too bad my evangelical kindergarten teacher made fun of me for wearing coats that didn't fit. Otherwise I might have been hurt.

their website, is "designed to introduce disinterested high-school kids to Jesus." They do so by enlisting club leaders with Goo Goo Dolls haircuts who can sell Christianity using their coolness by casually propping one leg onto a stool and telling horny teens, "Dude, God, like, doesn't want you to, like, have sex. Okay, man? In Jesus' name, cowabunga!"

The Young Life of West Houston was in a strip mall by 1-10 and Beltway 8. It was a scenic stretch of Houston surrounded by concrete supports, highways, and hopelessness. I went to one meeting with a boy named Mason who I was trying to lure into my vagina, my plan being to gain his trust by pretending to be a sweet virgin, then breaching his trust by sucking his dick under a pine tree. Meetings were held in a rectangular room, with zero art, off-white walls, and no chairs. Young Life wants to feel like a dope hang zone, but the vibe was more "front for Russian money-laundering cartel." The leader—a guy whose name I've forgotten but, safe bet, is probably Trey—kicked off the meeting with a transparency projector. He turned off the lights and everyone made an "ooooh" noise as if ANYONE IN THE ROOM WAS GETTING LAID. Mason was sitting next to me in his Texas uniform—crisp polo shirt, starched khakis, and boots. His eyes were glistening with excitement. What fun was in store for us tonight? Passing around a beach ball…INDOORS?! Free 7UP?!? Side hugs? Oh, it was much better than that. The light of the projector turned on, displaying the transparency on the wall with the lyrics to Bon Jovi's "Livin' on a Prayer." According to Jon Bon Jovi,[6] the song is about the effects of Reagan-era trickle-down economics on working-class families. But Young Life saw it as pop music bait to hook teens with hard-core Christianity.[7] As if any teen in the late '90s—the Hole and Smashing Pumpkins decade—was going to be like "WHAT?! Christians like decades'-old pop hits just like me, a teenager?!" Bon Jovi was not cool; it was the music choice of uncles who work out on Bowflexes in open garages while drinking beer, but when Trey pressed Play on the CD player, the whole room of virgins belted out the decades'-old megahit off of *Slippery When Wet*, an album clearly referencing what happened to pussies when they came close to Jon Bon Jovi and his home perm. The double entendre was lost on everyone but me.

This was just the kickoff of two hours of structured

---

6   When he's not onstage meltin' panties, he's hocking his dad's pasta sauce. Proceeds go to "combat issues that force families and individuals into economic despair," aka Tommy and Gina. The Jon Bon Jovi universe is a closed system.

7   All Bon Jovi songs have been fucked to more than they've been prayed to. That's what Jon Bon Jovi wants.

Christian fun. The whole thing was about as inspi-
rational as a dental hygienist showing me how to
floss each side of the tooth. During the club meeting
I suffered through, Trey's message of the night was
about our virginal promise to God and the importance of purity rings—the sterling silver wedding
rings teens wear to let everyone know their genitals
belong to Jesus, who's keeping them on ice until marriage. It was such a hard sell I almost expected to
see a jewelry rep step into the room with samples.
The whole speech was delivered with the energy
of someone trying to sell me a timeshare behind an
Exxon. It might shock you to find out that purity
rings are not a tradition going back to the *Mayflower*.
Christian abstinence groups handed 'em out like
candy in the '90s and the Treys of Young Life were
happy to keep the tradition going so young women
could nonverbally announce to the world, "My
pussy belongs to the Lord!"

Abstinence education, in any form, is astronom-
ically ineffective. Only 3 percent of the population
waits to have sex until they're married. The University of Massachusetts–Amherst found a whopping 30
percent of female teenage abstinence pledge takers
(and then breakers) got pregnant, compared to 18
percent of regular ol' sexually active teenagers. Of
course they did. They couldn't stop their horny zom-
bie bodies, and with no accurate knowledge about

safe, protected sex, they weren't aware of what could happen if their dude sprayed them down inside like a renegade garden hose.

If killjoy adults really wanted teens to stop having sex, they'd teach them how to masturbate. What they're doing isn't just about preventing intercourse; it's about control and deceit, and women bear the brunt of these malicious tactics. According to a Harvard report on abstinence education, titled "Sex, Lies & Stereotypes: How Abstinence-Only Programs Harm Women and Girls,"[8] young women are emotionally harmed by the idea that they are responsible for male sexuality. They also found women of color are more likely to get STDs from unprotected sex and that abstinence programs exacerbate racial inequality by propelling the stereotypes that black women are more sexually aggressive than white women and reinforcing traditional gender roles for Latinas. Abstinence education is a human rights issue for women and is a terrible amount of pressure and shame to put on an experience that means fuck all.

I lost my virginity to a guy named Bubba, and yeah, go ahead and judge, but it's not what you think. He wasn't some rotten-toothed exterminator in an

---

8   We've got a Steven Soderbergh fan at the Harvard School of Public Health!

American flag tank top, driving around in a jacked-up extended-cab pickup with balls hanging from the trailer hitch. Bubba was, improbably, an all-star football player with the body of Chris Evans, the smile of Idris Elba, and the brain of a fifth grader. And that last part is why he fucked me.

I'd been running a failed campaign my junior year to lose my virginity. The plan was to throw myself desperately at guys out of my league and see if anyone would take the bait. Hard-core flirting, getting detention for wearing butt crescent–revealing skirts to school, hanging on every word of a basketball player and laughing at his sentences even when they weren't jokes. For the late '90s, I was rocking a great look—overplucked eyebrows, old bowling shirts paired with short skirts, Dr. Martens, and brown lipstick. But once I opened my mouth, the secret was out: I was annoying.[9] My sophomore year I got kicked out of an Olive Garden for running around without shoes on, screaming and doing a joke where my bottom lip didn't work and so water would pour down my dress. A year may have passed, but that person, too classless for a restaurant chain that smells like a prison kitchen on meatball day, was still alive and well inside me. Even the horniest of teens

---

9   Also happens to be the casting description of every commercial
    role I've auditioned for.

didn't want the emotional mess that was five-foot-eleven me begging to be fucked. And then ding-dong hottie came to Houston for the summer. Bubba used to go to our junior high but moved back to Louisiana and was in Houston staying with his friend Robbie. My sister was dating Robbie and so I was around, and I guess Bubba liked how I hung on his every stupid word. I was new to him, which was good. He hadn't become absolutely unable to tolerate the sound of my voice.

One hot Houston summer night, Bubba took my virginity on the low-pile beige carpeting of my sister's bedroom.[10] Bubba was not a virgin, so I assumed he would know what he was doing, which was presumptuous. He didn't have a condom, so I gave him one—a hot-pink, old, probably defective condom I got in the bathroom of a tattoo parlor. After receiving my very first fake ID, I paid someone to tattoo terrible tribal art on my ankle with money I was supposed to use for a speeding ticket.[11] After the tattoo, I rewarded myself for being brave by buying a condom in the ladies'

---

10   Sorry, Audrey! Don't worry, I vacuumed afterward.
11   My dad wrote a genius letter making the argument that I didn't know I was speeding because we had just gotten a new car, a Bronco II, and the speedometer was different from our old car. Depending on the year of the car, the dead center of a speedometer might read 45, 60, or 80 or anywhere in between, and my armchair lawyer dad argued that I was not aware I was speeding because the indicator needle was exactly where it should have been in our old car for 15 mph.

room and telling myself I would put this on a special dick soon and have the night of my life. It was a night all right, and I experienced it while alive, but I wouldn't categorize it as "the night of my life." Bubba jammed his rubber-covered dick into my dry vagina and we sandpaper fucked until he was done.

I couldn't believe people had fun doing this. I'll admit, dry, awkward sex was better than an orgasm from rocking my Levi's 501 crotch seam back and forth against a beanbag chair, but not by much. Losing my virginity was like being promised my whole life that, one special day, I'd eat the best pizza in all of Italy, and then, when the special day arrived, I was handed an overcooked pepperoni Hot Pocket.

First times are always disappointing. Which is why people need to practice. So let's save the $75 billion we put into abstinence education each year and give teens reversible vasectomies, a warehouse full of condoms, a full understanding of consent, and then set them free to go to town on each other's perfect bodies God filled with gallons of hormones. To suck and lick and fuck and experiment with whoever they want and make mistakes and get better. So by the time they're in their twenties everyone's all, like, *really* good at sex and there won't be *Hunger Games*–style fights between girlfriends over Carlos on our improv team because we've heard he fucks like a champion.

DOCTORS ARE NOT THE BOSS
OF YOU

Picture this: 2003, Houston is in the throes of a classic Gulf of Mexico Thanksgiving. The trees are dead, the rain is relentless, and all of my worst high school friends are spending their nights at Pennison's sports pub as a joke, doing peppermint schnapps shots and talking about the "good ol' days," which were only six years ago. I'm home from Chicago, where I've been living on my own far away from Houston for the first time since college. I've traded in Coldplay for the Shins, Dave Matthews for the Strokes. I'm different and I don't care to be around a bunch of people who will make fun of me for having a better haircut and reading books for fun. They can throw up minty liquor all night; I won't be around to see it. I'm in the *Looking for Mr. Goodbar* portion of my twenties, full of independence and stupidity, trading the familiarity of friends for the company of strangers. I was at a dive bar in Montrose—the "cool" part of Houston—by myself, reading Spalding Gray's *Swimming to Cambodia*, purposefully holding the cover up to see if anyone at the Snake Pit was buying my newly acquired sophistication.

"Oh, look at her, a young hottie in a little boy's Old Navy flannel shirt reading a book and drinking wine. Her arms are more muscular than most women's but I like that. She looks like the kind of woman who thinks *It's a Wonderful Life* is overrated. I hope it's true," he would think. He being Declan, who rolls his tattered copy of Immanuel Kant's *Critique of Pure Reason* into the back pocket of his perfectly fitted '70s Levi's. He grabs his whiskey and adjusts his semi-wrinkled blue oxford shirt and walks toward me. "What are two people like us doing in such a dumpster fire of a city?" he'd ask. Then we'd both respond, "Visiting." Oh we'd laugh and laugh. We'd make love like wild dogs and it would never ever get old. I imagined our East Village apartment, littered with fiddle leaf figs and old records of bands who had long since been forgotten. Dinner parties of bone marrow and fresh brioche from the baker under our building. Our credit card bill would arrive and we'd laugh. "How can we ever pay off the $65,000 we spent keeping up this lifestyle?" We'd laugh some more, then do a bunch of drugs. We're fun together.

Declan never came but Farhad did. Interested in my childish attire and adultish reading habits, or just straight-up horny, he chatted me up at the bar. Also visiting for the holiday, he was hanging out with a friend who promptly got lost after a half hour of standing behind us as we flirted. Farhad was very fit and very handsome and very smart and a head and neck surgeon, which blew me away. I can't imagine the amount of things one would have to know to even begin to understand the head. The neck sounds pretty easy; it's a spine and a tube and a couple of boxing bags hanging from the throat. But still, if someone came to me with a neck problem, I wouldn't know where to start. All I knew was you had to be smart to be a doctor, and then double smart to be a specific kind of doctor. Looked like I hit the jackpot.

After making out on barstools at the Snake Pit like two drunk slobs, we rented a hotel room at the DoubleTree—the only hotel for a hookup where you're guaranteed a warm cookie. We were naked, and I was about to mount him like a Clydesdale when he stopped me. Farhad explained he was scared I might hurt his dick. Once, while a woman was riding him cowgirl, she bent his dick back with the entire weight of her torso. He was overly concerned I be wet enough to execute the routine flawlessly. At this point, I'd had ten vodkas and a pack of American Spirit cigarettes. My body wasn't working like she should and I didn't want to cause further injury to the poor doctor's penis. How can he go back to work saving headnecks with a broken dick clanging around in his scrubs? I couldn't have that on my conscience. Thankfully, the good doctor came up with a medical solution: I should squirt hotel conditioner up my vagina!

And I didn't even QUESTION IT. He went to medical school! Surely there was an entire SEMESTER devoted to the safety of mixing panthenol, silicone, and humectants with the delicate pH balance of the most complicated organ on planet Earth! Hotel conditioner doesn't exit the bottle like home conditioner does. It doesn't delicately slide from the pump like a follicle-nourishing liquid silk; it plops out like old sour cream, in tiny little globules of hair-softening goop. I violently ejected the thick substance from the miniature bottle and rubbed it inside my baby canal. Conditioner in the vagina feels exactly like you think it would—like a thin coating of heavily perfumed yogurt. I smeared the rest of the contents onto Farhad's semierect manhood and slipslided all up and down him, not injuring his dick in any way.

For nearly a week, my insides rid itself of the foreign substance, spitting out little bits of conditioner into my panties. During this fight for cleanliness, my lady parts were attacked by a yeast infection more powerful than all the kombucha mothers in San Francisco combined. How could a *doctor* do this to me?

There's a misconception about doctors. Just because a person has the guts to dissect a corpse for eleventy billion hours does not automatically transform them into some sort of all-knowing superbeing who has the definitive answers to all human conditions.[1] And sure, that's okay if you're just hooking up with a doctor who convinces you to shove hair care products up your naughty bits, but what if you're in their office and you need actual medical advice?

For about seven years, I went to a very prominent gynecologist in Los Angeles. It was an accident that I saw him in the first place; he has a gender-neutral first name, which I assumed meant a jaunty woman filled with a love of gardening and a deep devotion to medical well-being would enter the exam room. It's important to be comfortable with your gynecologist because it's a very intimate doctor's visit. For those of you reading this book who have never had a well woman's exam, let me explain what happens.

First, we get completely nude. Then we slip on

---

1   I'm not saying all doctors should be approached with a healthy level of distrust, but it can't hurt. The good ones will put you at ease quickly; the bad ones will be easier to spot.

a paper bolero jacket, our breasts exposed but our shoulders and back completely covered, ya know, so we feel comfortable. The frosty air-conditioning blows across our bare breasts, creating tiny little icicles that hang from our nipples—nipcicles if you will. Then we unfold a paper blanket so thin it makes an airplane throw look like a luxury goose down comforter and drape it over our legs and pelvis. We sit in our paper towel shroud for forty-five minutes to two hours, reading a 2016 *People* magazine. Are Miley Cyrus and Liam Hemsworth engaged? Then our doctor walks in. For those of us who have not been pregnant, a gynecologist is essentially a stranger who we see once a year for twenty minutes. There are no apologies for their lateness. You scoot your butt down to the edge of the table and put your legs into two little Tiny Tim leg braces; then the doctor unceremoniously shoves a cold, wet metal caulking gun into your vagina like it's no big deal. A Q-tip the size of a baseball bat is inserted and rubbed on your cervix and then sent to the lab for tests. They release the metal opener, but it's not over! They put one entire hand inside your vagina, then the other on your stomach and press them together to see if they can touch, because that's apparently the best way to investigate a uterus in the twenty-first century. The whole thing ends with a breast exam, sometimes a rectal exam, and then it's 364 days until the fun starts again.

I don't have anything personal against straight male gynecologists other than I find their career choice suspect as fuck. I am sure there are like four sexless guys in obstetrics and gynecology, but I've had SEVERAL boyfriends who couldn't go to yoga class because they would get erections from seeing the outline of women's coochies in downdog, so I'm thinking it's entirely possible a lot of these dudes are in the vagina biz for weird reasons.[2]

I'm a polite Southerner whose first instinct is always to spare other people's feelings over my own comfort, so instead of leaving when I saw this Stephen Colbert/Bob Saget face-mash enter the room, I let this man examine me. Things were fine with Mr. Keepin' That Gender Vague for three or so years. Then in 2010, I'm using my paper-gown hour to work on a book proposal—a comedic essay book about sex I did not sell because I was a hundred years late to that game—in he bursts, no apologies, and sees my laptop, piquing his interest. I know by his waiting room he's pulling in real Hollywood B-listers, so I'm not shocked at how nosy he is about my work. When I tell him what I'm writing, he asks, "Am I in it?"

---

2   Do you remember what Cliff Huxtable's job was on the *Cosby Show*? He had an ob-gyn practice in his home basement. He was a basement gynecologist!

"Why would you be in it?"[3] I asked, confused. Why would I talk about my gynecologist in a book about all the losers I fucked? The nurse-practitioner who chaperones him during visits didn't react.[4] I let it go. I only saw this guy once a year, so I could deal with this in small doses. Plus, finding a new gynecologist is like trying to catch a friend up on a show they've never seen during the season finale; I just don't have the time. The next year, he tried to talk me out of the preventative mastectomy I talked about earlier. His office had a gigantic photo-realistic oil painting of a baby being pulled out of a woman via C-section. The artist had drawn a spotlight around this kid, terrified and covered in pregnancy slime, and the doctor had framed the monstrosity with the kind of ornate woodwork you'd find around Raphael's *Sistine Madonna*. I stared at it. "You know I don't want children, right? I've mentioned it several times," I added.

"Women always change their minds."

This is the kind of stuff you write for a villain to

---

3   Guess he got what he wanted, to be in my book ;) Probably not for the reasons he wanted ;)

4   Guess who doesn't need a nurse-practitioner in her examining room? My new gynecologist, Dr. Susan Morrison. 'Cause she's not afraid she's gonna say some inappropriate garbage to me while my bare butt is pressing into white butcher paper.

say, so later, when he's hanging off a cliff, you can watch the heroine stomp on his fingers with her heels and feel that justice has been served.

And yes, I did make an appointment that day for a follow-up in a year. In addition to the yearly Pap, I wanted to get an IUD. My friend loved hers and I was dating my now husband, who I was having lots of sex with but didn't quite know if we were going to work out. Our decorating styles are wildly different and he didn't use a calendar then, so I wasn't sure I could count on him to show up on the right day of an abortion. I made an appointment with Dr. Can't Believe You're Still Seeing Me to have him shove a skinny, upside-down baby-preventing anchor into my uterus. When he inserted it, he accidentally punched it into the top of my uterus.[5] Imagine the pain of a thousand jellyfish concentrated into one area deep inside the most sensitive part of your body. Then magnify that agony by one thousand and you'll sort of understand what kind of distress I was in. The misery was so intense, my brain did everyone

---

5   Dr. Susan Morrison, an angel sent from heaven to rescue me from lady doctor hell, found out that I have a heart-shaped uterus, and that's why the IUD insertion process was so painful. It also means that it's hard for me to have a baby, for which I am grateful. I never wanted to have kids and now when people ask me if Ale and I are having kids, I say, "My uterus is deformed," and enjoy their looks of embarrassment. Teach those bitches a lesson in minding their own business.

a favor and passed me out. When I woke up, I could barely walk. My balance was off and I was sick from the pain. Dr. Uterus Punch apologized and ran out of the room like a coward, leaving me with the nurse-practitioner, who was sympathetic but offered me no explanations about what the fuck was happening. All she knew was most people don't react like this. When I stopped passing out, I was allowed to DRIVE MYSELF HOME, sitting in an upright car seat, compressing the part of my body that had just been traumatized. I crawled into bed and cried. For dinner, I ordered in Indian food from a new place and it was not good, topping off an F-minus day with a runny masala. It took me two days to recover, but I still wasn't fully back to normal. Every time I sat in a chair, that tiny little contraption jabbed me, reminding me it's still there and still pointy. After a month of a living nightmare, I went in to have the stupid thing removed. "Are you sure you want it out? Sometimes it takes a couple of months to settle in," Dr. Women Don't Know Anything asked me, AFTER I had listed all the reasons it was not welcome inside me. "Take it out today!"[6] He was scared because I was mad. It took me years to get slightly angry with this motherfucker, and on this day, he would

---

6   I got a full refund. Which means they knew they fucked up something.

do something that would push my experience with anger into a whole new horizon.

The nurse-practitioner, who, let's be honest, always does the real work, put me in a robe and stuck my feet into the stirrups, while the doctor grabbed a removal tool. It resembled metal tongs, the kind you lower corn into boiling water with, only thinner and three times as long. I saw his head disappear under the horizon line created by the paper sheet draped between my two legs. I could sort of feel what was going on inside me but it was too vague to make out exactly what was happening. The internal movement stopped. From below my paper gown, an IUD, covered in blood and uterus ooze, appeared, and then I heard, in a high-pitched cartoon voice, this:

"I'M OUT! I'M OUT!!!"

It was the puppet show no one asked for, voiced by a medical professional hiding underneath my throwaway garment, his face inches away from my pussy, smiling and having a great time. He had to hide his face. It was necessary; otherwise it would have destroyed the illusion the IUD was alive.

When he realized I didn't appreciate his brand of theater, he popped his head over my opened legs and smiled. "All better!" With that, they both left the room…without a curtain call! Where would I throw my roses? I lay there for, I dunno, six years, and thought about what just happened. There was only one way to handle this. I immediately marched out of there and confronted him. Did he think because I am in the comedy business I enjoy jokes when I'm in a vulnerable situation at the DOCTOR'S, nude, with my legs wide open? I don't care how many celebrity babies he's plucked out of *This Is Us* costars; I won't be treated so casually. This might be Hollywood—number one enemy of women—but I demand that in this office I am treated with dignity and respect![7]

Just kidding: I said nothing and saw him for another two years. While I was telling someone my hilarious Dr. Carrot Top Prop Comedian OBJokesYN story, my friend Rachel, who cares about me and is so tired of this story—even though it kills at parties—BEGGED me to have some self-respect and switch to her doctor. And I did. In early 2016, I went in to

---

7   Okay, if straight men want to be gynecologists, they have to agree to these three rules:
    1. They have to pay for a woman to follow them around at all times—even outside of work—for a year, to correct all inappropriate behavior. She'll keep an Excel spreadsheet of all his mistakes and have it at the ready to use as a threat.
    2. If the reason they went into gynecology is that they were raised and surrounded by strong women, prove it. Like I want to see a wall covered with auntie photos. I want to lie on your examination table and look up at the ceiling and see a picture of your mom giving me a thumbs-up.
    3. They have to punch themselves in the dick before every exam. I want their dicks to associate a stinging pain with exposed labia. When their dick sees a pussy, I want it to be scared.

see her gay male ob-gyn, who told me he didn't think a woman should be president until after she's been through menopause. Ya know, 'cause of all the hormones. He picked the perfect time to tell me, as he was checking my ovaries from the inside of my butthole. This guy was a step up for me!

These are all doctors who are trained by schools for a long time to deal specifically with women and they can't even do that right. So, it stands to reason if the medical experts who are supposed to know everything about women are failing, medical nonexperts are probably committing untold atrocities.

Even though for years doctors study the physiological ways men and women are different, we are treated medically as if we're the same. Textbooks are partly to blame. According to the study "Sexism in Anatomy" published in the *Journal of Anatomy*, many medical textbooks lack illustrations of the female body, which means med students can't even find the clitoris!! I understand the female system is way more complicated and there's more to learn about, but, um, so what? It's medical school. If ya want an easy degree, study fashion merchandising like I did. I spent nearly an entire semester in the Houston Galleria critiquing Gucci window displays and memorizing different kinds of lightbulbs. Sometimes I would drink margaritas and eat southwestern egg rolls at the Cheesecake Factory and watch people learn to ice-skate and then in ten minutes, finish my lesson, drunk.

It's also hard to find good data on how medicine affects women because we've only been allowed to participate in clinical trials since 1993, when the FDA decided it might be important to find out how drugs affect us differently. But even with the FDA's permission, we're still left out of a lot of research because of our period.

"The complexities of the menstrual cycle are considered major barriers to the inclusion of women in clinical trials," argue the researchers behind a 2016 editorial published in the *British Journal of Sports Medicine*. The complexities of the menstrual cycle are barriers to many things—wearing white pants with confidence, entering Balinese temples, sex without a towel. And now medical studies. Here's why it's important to test medicine on people with different physiological components. Because of what happened with Ambien.

We've all heard about some of the crazy shit people do while in an Ambien sleep trance. My friend Caroline, who is in her midtwenties, will wake up the morning after Ambien to find an email confirming her order of some Home Shopping nonsense purchase of like seven bottles of Carol's Daughter Hair Milk she has no recollection of buying. Ambien turns my friend Caroline into a bored sixty-eight-year-old woman recovering from hip surgery. Hallucinations, "sleep driving," which is dangerous and sometimes deadly, and sending emails that just read "hhhjnnnnnnngggg," are all side effects of Ambien. But Japanese researchers have noted women were more likely to suffer from these severe side effects compared to men. The FDA didn't pay attention to their study until Kai Falkenberg wrote about the phenomenon in *Marie Claire* in 2013. Then another study was released by the Substance Abuse and Mental Health Services Administration reporting women accounted for two-thirds of the Ambien-related emergency room visits. After all that, the FDA[8] *finally* lowered the dosage recommendation for women.

Women are also twice as likely to have bad reactions to medicine and we're affected differently by a whole slew of psychotropic medications. We're less likely to be properly treated for fibromyalgia, which is basically a lady disease. And, big one here, women are more likely to be misdiagnosed when we're having a heart attack because we often experience symptoms other than chest pain, like shortness of breath, cold sweats, and jaw pain, aka how I feel

---

8   The FDA isn't exactly known for its lightning-fast reflexes; it still enforces a ban on accepting donated blood from sexually active gay men despite the fact that all blood started being screened for HIV seven Cher albums ago.

after a premenstrual In-N-Out French fry bender. Seems like it would be easy enough for doctors to update the Rolodex of symptoms they carry around in their brains, but the stereotype of a man grabbing his chest while he falls to the ground is difficult to, uh, kill.

Of course, all this medical negligence is worse if you're a black woman. The United States already has a high maternal mortality rate, very high for a developed country, and one of the reasons is that black mothers die at three to four times the rate of white mothers, according to a report by NPR. The institutionalized sexism in the medical profession puts on a racism hat and does a little dance before it treats black women. All women suffer from their pain not being taken seriously by doctors, but black women more so. Black and Hispanic patients across the board are less likely to receive adequate treatment for their pain. Even Serena Williams goes through this shit! In a 2017 *Vogue* interview, she spoke about how she's prone to blood clots and how, after she gave birth, she was having trouble breathing and assumed she was experiencing a clot in her lungs. She told a nurse what was happening but this fuckin' nurse suggested to Williams that her pain medication must be making her confused. Williams eventually received the CT scan she requested, and it confirmed she wasn't making it up. Because of course she wasn't; Serena knows her body! She shouldn't have to harangue a team of medical staff to pay attention to her just because she's a black woman.

GET IT TOGETHER, MEDICAL INDUSTRY! Considering how to treat women's health shouldn't be an afterthought. And for my lady patient friends, start treating your doctors[9] like your Trump-supporting, Facebook-headline-skimming aunt. Make them explain what they're saying to you. Make them cite their sources. Make them communicate. Explain that Hillary was cleared of any wrongdoing multiple times. Be the exhausting bitch who is out there advocating for your health and when you don't like the answers, their attitude, and the way they're treating you, pull out your phone in front of them, press your home button, and say, "Siri, call the state medical board complaint hotline"[10] and as you wait on hold, look the doctor straight in the eyes and say, "I didn't take no hippocratic oath to first do no harm."

---

9   Of course, if you have a great doctor, give her a hug and tell her she's special and you appreciate her, and ask if she knows how we can clone her.

10   California's State Medical Complaint Number is 1-800-633-2322 and the motto on their website is "Don't Wait, File a Complaint!" Exclamation points theirs.

TURNING THAT STD UPSIDE DOWN

There's a kool klub you may or may not be a part of. It's a fun rager for the fucking raddest chicks in the world. The party is called genital herpes—and if you're not one of the twenty-six million U.S. women who have it, where you at, SISTER? Your STDs are waiting for you![1] If your pussy is cleaner than Clorox Clean-Up, lemme tell you how to get totally invaded by the most popular STD, like, ever!

Getting herpes is not easy. It took me years! You can't just rub your poonany on an uncovered Penn Station toilet seat; you have to train and be methodical if you want to do it right.

---

1   Some of you might already be BFFs with herpes and don't even know it; 85 percent of people with herpes find out they have it when it rips through their body like a tiny man pickaxing through genital skin.

The first thing you have to do is be absolutely stupid.[2] If you were homeschooled by evangelical parents, congratulations, you are WAY ahead of the game! Not that American public schools are cranking out sex-ed experts. My high school sex-ed class was taught by a baseball coach who stammered out anatomical terms like *vagina* and *penis*, sweat dripping down his forehead like he'd just seen the ghost of a Civil War soldier floating through the classroom. I'm just saying, if the man had been having a stroke in front of us, no one would have noticed the difference. My parents didn't tell me anything either. The only person who was there to help us kids understand our biscuits and sausages was Devin Taylor's older gay brother. He gave us a copy of *Kids*, a deranged movie about New York City teens who fuck and do drugs and give each other HIV. We'd rotate houses for regular viewing parties, and a room full of teenagers would suddenly go quiet, watching, slack jawed, as these misfits used sex as a tool of anarchy. *Kids* is totally insane and broke every child indecency law in America, but we finally had some answers! We found out where we could go to get tested for STDs, what reckless bare-

---

2   I'm just saying you probably won't get herpes if you're one of those peeps who checked the CDC website every time they recall a bag of salad. Those paranoid pansies are too busy Purelling guys' dicks to get themselves virused.

backing looked like, that slut-shaming hurts, and how people without legs ride skateboards. Learning I could get AIDS from one sexual encounter, then give it to a guy who is raping me while I'm passed out on drugs at a house party was valuable information for me and my sexually active friends. Do you think I kept fucking my boyfriend condomless in the bathroom[3] at house parties? Not after *Kids* I didn't. But my education was limited to what was covered in that movie. If Larry Clark[4] didn't shoot it, I didn't know it. Which meant I still didn't know a lot.

In college, I learned nothing new about STDs but I did learn even in college no one wanted to fuck me. So I kept fucking Bubba, the guy to whom I lost my virginity. I would drive six hours to New Orleans to have sex with him only to have him ditch me in the middle of Bourbon Street for hours while he ran off and got drunk with his friends and laughed at trans strippers. Dude was a complete goon. Eventually I stopped wasting my gas money driving to another state for sex with that lunkhead. Ugh, that whole time, from college until my marriage at twenty-five, was awful. How could I learn

---

3   I'm shocked I don't have permanent spine damage from being fucked into the sink faucet.

4   I'm not a fan of Larry Clark, but I appreciate that he put something out there that kept me from getting AIDS.

about sexual health and safety? I was deeply depressed about whether or not I could actually date someone I liked in Texas. I was a young, liberal, loud woman with a deep love of silly jokes and an overactive sense of righteousness trying to date in a state full of guys in Tommy Hilfiger shirts and Red Wing boots who like their women quiet and agreeable.

Then, at twenty-four, I met my first husband through a friend who used to live in LA. He's Jewish, smart, in the entertainment industry, and super fit, nothing like any of the guys I had ever met. We got married two months after we met and after we both had STD tests that came back negative, so I didn't have to keep learning about that shit! I was out of the system! When we got divorced, even though it was the right thing, I fell into a deep depression. The only things I had an appetite for were plain chicken breasts and cigarettes, transforming my body into a lithe, sexy skeleton. Before I was ready, I got back into the dating cesspool to look for some new dick to dock. This was pre-Tinder, so it was on to OkCupid where I, elbowmodel, searched for people to fill my emotional and physical hole: the grad student studying architecture at UCLA, the coder with two earrings in each lobe, the writer, the other writer, a THIRD WRITER! None of them gave me herpes! Then I met Krunlap

Von Swingleton[5] in an acting class. Krunlap was a very, very impossibly good-looking professional stand-up, a unicorn in the comedy world. Be truly honest with yourself when you think you're attracted to a male comic. Remove the stage and the jokes, if you saw an unevenly shaved dude eating a burrito from the inside out at 3:00 a.m. like a crow chowing down on a squirrel carcass, in between intermittent cocaine phlegm collections, you would absolutely run in the other direction. Krunlap flirted with me in class, and I flirted back. We got to know each other through cold readings and after-class hangouts. When I found out he paid out of pocket to have his teeth cleaned three times a year, I soaked my chair.

Most male stand-ups are real slut bags[6] and Krunlap was no different. Fucking women in Tucson and Buffalo, doing blow with his opener in San Diego, then banging whatever low-hanging fruit was misguided enough to believe a night in a sperm-crusted hotel room paid for by the Laff Shack was going to change her life.

Krunlap possessed a potent, Catholic, people-pleasing drive and a borderline-homicidal sexual appetite, making him the perfect fuck machine. One

---

5   Not his name. I hope not anyone's name.
6   Even the dorks. ESPECIALLY the dorks.

night, I was sitting on his face, wishing I could freeze time and stay there forever. Was there a way to put his face on an ergonomic office chair? Could I market it as the Krunlap Cunnilingus Herman Miller chair? Little did I know, as I contacted imaginary venture capitalists in my head, that my herpes club card was on its way.

A couple days later, I was shooting a commercial when I was struck with genital pain I can only describe as a thousand Thumbelinas starting campfires on my labia. In the bathroom I discovered the horror in my panties; my skin had ripped open—in a popped blister kind of way—making the most sensitive parts of my body burn with agony. It looked like my labia were a butterfly emerging from a skin cocoon—but replace "butterfly" with "exposed, raw, infected vagina flesh." Not something you want landing on your children's nose in a natural history pavilion. I couldn't leave the shoot. There are no emergencies in acting when you only make money four times a year. So, I suffered through what I thought was a staph infection from waxing by running to the bathroom every time someone called "Cut!," sitting on an industrial toilet and pouring Arrowhead water down my jellyfish-stanged cooter. Then I dried off and went back to set and did my job like Judy Fucking Garland would have.

We wrapped at 6:00 p.m. and it was Friday, so my

gyno was already on his way home in his fancy car to practice his IUD cartoon voices. As bad as my gyno was/is, he was nothing compared to the dumbass doctor[7] I saw at the ER at Cedars-Sinai. He was looking at my vagina as if damaged human parts weren't his expertise. This guy had no idea—after all those years in medical school—that I was suffering from the most common STD in America. Here's how I know he didn't know. If he *did* know those lesions were herpes, and painful, he wouldn't have given me a PELVIC EXAM like a fucking masochist. Was I at a hospital or inside Dick Cheney's Guantanamo wet dream? Doctor Garbage Brains proceeded to pull out a speculum, which is not the tool of choice for someone whose clamchops looked like they've been fingered by Edward Scissorhands. It's normally uncomfortable, but opening the speculum also tore open the exposed, bright-red finger lakes decorating my salami garage. I have a high threshold for pain thanks to previously mentioned years of my mom's aggressive ponytail-styling methods, but this made me pass out. Dr. Demented sent me home with amoxicillin and a pat on the shoulder. I'm just glad I got out of there before he put a potato sack over

---

7   Not all ER doctors are awful. I had a very nice one in college when I was sick with swollen adenoids in College Station, Texas. I'll never forget him. His name was That Doctor Once in College.

my head and waterboarded me. The only way I got through the weekend was thanks to my responsible prescription-drug-addict friends. They'd drop off tiny ziplock bags of the stuff at my doorstep and I would crack open my front door, extend my claw, and pull the random pills inside. Then I would slide into a saltwater bath like a salamander and stay there until Monday, when my gyno could finally see me.

Turns out the only time my gynecologist is serious is when there's an actual medical problem. He didn't have any jokes like "Ouch! Whadya do? Sit on a table saw?" or "Looks like somebody needs some Blisterine!" Instead, he put on his human being face and broke the news to me that I probably had herpes. "It's not possible—we always wear a condom!" I yelled. Then I cried. I cried so hard. He explained condoms don't protect against herpes. Even though Krunlap the Sex Addict Comedian always wore a condom, turns out his teeth cleanings weren't keeping his mouth that clean. According to medical science—that's apparently only taught to three doctors and no non-doctors—if you rub your fuck-torn goop chute on the face of a guy who had chickenpox as a kid and who now gets cold sores on his adult mouth, then CONGRATUFUCKINGLATIONS, you have herpes!! There are so many other ways to get herpes; this was just the method easiest for me. Feel free to adjust according to what method works for you—fucking a five-time-divorced Major League Baseball player bareback, letting any member of a Coldplay cover band go down on you, rimming a comic book store owner with a ponytail and a crustache, you get it.

So, now you've got herpes! Welcome to the Valtrex jungle. But what do you do now with your newfound sores? (Besides brag.) At first, you're gonna want to spit in your Krunlap's face after screaming, "You selfish pile of elephant diarrhea!" while in the middle of Sycamore Kitchen, interrupting everyone's morning avocado toast. And that's fine. Get it out of your system. It will be hard to do when he tells you he *might* have done this to a previous girlfriend who he *thinks* was also misdiagnosed by an emergency room in Los Angeles and hearing you explain the situation he can clearly see that probably *was* the case and so now you find yourself on a call with a person you are furious at while also begging him to immediately call his ex-girlfriend so he can break the news to her that she has herpes. Then order your scrambled eggs with chorizo, hide in the corner where no one will notice if you're crying, and focus on what it means to now be STD'ed.

The scariest aspect for women, a group already overloaded with blame about their sexuality, is that the shame associated with herpes gets magnified. We think, "Oh, okay, I was acting like a motherfucking dick pig, so of course I deserve to get an STD" instead of understanding promiscuity has nothing to do with getting an STD. Jenelle Marie Davis, founder of the STD Project, told Mic.com that outside of the internalized turmoil we feel, a woman's status can be used against her because men will "think these women will just be thankful that someone is there for them and somebody is just accepting their infection." When women believe they have no other options, they might stay in relationships that are unhealthy because they feel no one else will love them. The world has been reinforcing this terribly lopsided stigma since the ancient Greeks, when Antigone hanged herself in her tomb after Hæmon gave her the herp.

One of my first post-herpes hook-ups was with a real estate agent I bumped into in a saccharine meet-cute while riding in a Beverly Hills elevator. Later that night, at my apartment, I let him know about my plagued pussy and he was so nice about turning me down for sex. He explained he was "squeamish about germs and that stuff." Then he begged me to dress up like a baby and drink his cum out of a bottle. Which I did NOT do, but I *did* let him hyperventilate into my butthole, which isn't a method of herpes transmission according to the Centers for Disease Control and Prevention (CDC). This dude was very much the exception, though; most people are (a) not as open about their adult baby fetishes on the first date and (b) much cooler about your "big" herpes admission. To protect myself, I made new rules for dating. Instead of just fucking whatever dick came my way, I invested more time in men I liked and cut the dead weight off early. I did not suffer anyone who didn't deserve my fourth-date "I have herpes" talk. I got to know the person with their clothes on, lowering my chances of being pushed away by some heartless monster.

On top of the special shame women feel, STDs have the added bonus of impacting women more physiologically. The American Sexual Health Association has a depressing list on their website of all the ways women are impacted more by sexually transmitted diseases than men. For example, we're more likely to contract STDs because compared to the thick skin of a dick, we have sweet, delicate vagina skin that just can't help but take in bacteria and infection. Why do guys get everything: political power, bigger earning potential, thicker genital skin?! When women do honey trap something, like chlamydia or gonorrhea, symptoms might not show up as fast as they do in guys, and gone untreated could result in pelvic inflammatory disease, which is a catch-all for a kaleidoscope of things that could go wrong with your baby maker and impact fertility and pregnancy. The only thing I'm giving birth to is a rogue tampon or an archival dollop of hotel conditioner, so I got no worries in that department.

"Stop STDs," a study by Quest Diagnostics, a lab processing everyone's dirty little sexually transmitted cotton swabs, sought to learn more about young women's attitudes on STDs. Out of the eighteen to twenty-four-year-olds they spoke to, only 56 percent said they'd been tested. That number is low because of two factors: 27 percent reported they didn't feel comfortable talking about sex or lied about their sex life when speaking to their doctor and half of them said their doctor never asked them if they wanted to be tested.[8] Whatever the reason women aren't getting tested, there are other ways to get an STD test that don't involve talking to a doctor IRL or depending on a doctor to do the right thing, two things that absolutely need to change, but I can't wave a magic wand and make everyone do the right thing all at once. If I could I would get people in LA to pull all the way up to the end of the curb when street parking. Four cars can park on this block, Tuscon-tourist-used-to-having-ample-curb-space! There are at-home STD tests (Everlywell, MyLabBox) you can do/take/swab in the comfort of your garden tub. If you then find out you have something rumbling down under, find a doctor in your area who is an STD specialist. In a cursory Internet search for LA

8　The CDC mandates that a clinician ask patients yearly if they want to have an STD panel run, even if they don't see symptoms.

genital infection experts I found a bunch of people BRAGGING about how ready they are to fix whatever ails your sick sugar walls. Most of these diseases—chlamydia, gonorrhea, syphilis, scabies, crabs, and something called trichomoniasis[9]—can all be treated with antibiotics. For the ones you have 4LYFE, like herpes, there are treatments for the symptoms, like my big ole bottle of Valtrex I keep handy. Although since I was unceremoniously infected, I've only had one breakout in five years, so next time I need it I'll get the added drama of having to blow a thick layer of dust off the bottle like a mad scientist. That's gonna be fun.

The best way to deal with having herpes is to operate as if everyone has it, 'cause many people do. The World Health Organization reported in 2015 that over half a billion people have genital herpes, so next time you hear someone making a herpes joke, let him know most of the room is not laughing.

The most important thing we as women have to do is start talking about our sexual diseases honestly. If not for you, then for other women. I was at a female-only writing retreat in Palm Springs that I hate to bring up because the septic system backed

---

9   I hope it's called "tricky" for short. "Yeah, I got the tricky. You?"

up the first night and when I got out of bed the next morning I put my foot right into sloshy, poop water–soaked carpet. But the *good* thing that came out of the trip was the night before I was talking through issues I was having writing this chapter, and one of the women stopped me. "Krunlap gave you herpes? Krunlap Von Swingleton? Oh, no, he dated my roommate last year." Then she called her roommate to tell her she might have herpes. Because if Krunlap[10] is too chickenshit to tell women he has herpes before he chomps on their pussies, at least my loud mouth will get them to the doctor.[11]

If you have herpes, don't despair; it doesn't mean you're a slut or damaged goods. If someone doesn't want to date you because of herpes, you're not the problem, they are. Having herpes means you're fun. It means you're an adult. It means you're an American, goddamnit! Take your Valtrex prescription to the CVS on La Cienega and watch as everyone in

---

10 If you see me in person, I will tell you his real name, but I am not putting it in this book because I legally can't. Until you can get me in private, never ever sleep with a touring male comedian.

11 Doctors don't test for herpes when you get a full STD panel; the CDC doesn't recommend it unless a patient says they're experiencing symptoms because it could come up negative if your herpes is hibernating like an American brown bear. But fuck those jerks. What you need to do is ask for the PRC blood test, which looks for the virus's DNA without presenting an outbreak, and get some meds so you are ready if the storm hits.

line checks out the new woman on the block. No slumped-over shame walk necessary. Strut in like Naomi Campbell power stomping down the runway, and if anyone looks at you sideways, throw your phone at them.

YOU ARE MORE THAN
YOUR TANK TOP

There's a major part of film history everybody gets wrong. In *The Wizard of Oz*, when the Wicked Witch of the West threatens Dorothy with "I'll get you, my pretty," it's not because that naive broad stole her ruby slippers. It's because Dorothy stupidly paired them with a casual picnic dress.

Green Face was right to be mad! Women's clothing must be regulated. Think about where this world would be without guidelines—scientists would be blowing up labs, cars would be crashing into each other, and women would be free to wear whatever we want, and we just can't have that kind of chaos!

There's no higher power to save us the humiliation of a fashion misstep or a high-tech mirror with the voice of a benevolent Anna Wintour saying in a monotone robot voice, "You're leaving the house in *that?*" So we must step boldly into the outside world, every day, waiting for the rules to be revealed to us as we fail.

But I would like to, at the very least, *attempt* an outline of all the rules dictating how women should dress in every situation—so we don't, you know, disrupt the delicate balance of society. This chapter is composed of real-life examples of situations where someone had a problem with something a woman wore, and then put her through the clothes wringer for it.

Let's start with news anchors. You know the news—where people in suits tell us about yesterday's Internet. KTLA5's meteorologist Liberté Chan was doing her regular weather report for Los Angeles—something like "Looks like another day of desolate garbage-fire smell and unrelenting cancerous sunshine for Southern California today"[1]— while wearing a sparkly, sleeveless black dress. Now, I know sleeveless apparel is a no-go for certain dark corners of corporate America. Those ancient buildings where smiling means you're weak and birthday cake sing-alongs in the kitchen are the only time you see Harvey from logistics feel joy. Where everything smells like old boat wood and the men in charge

---

1 Other reports in that day's newscast were on a coyote signing an overall deal with Netflix and the opening of LA's one millionth poke bar.

have ear hair shaped like cotton candy. Where HR is GOD! and stealing staples is a federal offense and "no, you can't have a space heater, Tonya! I don't care that you're shivering; it's a fire hazard!" In these Dickensian workplaces, the dress code would never allow a bare shoulder, because the formidable power of a woman's uncovered top arm can grind Cadwalader, Wickersham & Taft to a dramatic halt. All those soft boners in moldy suits, unable to concentrate because of the unbridled sexual power of three square inches of skin. But Liberté Chan works in SoCal, baby! Black sleeveless dresses are for square conservatives, dude! I assume anyone in LA whose butt creases are covered or under-boob is hidden is on their way to a Westboro Baptist Church jubilee. So I don't know from whence the Liberté Chan hater train came, but come it did. There was a lot to be said about Liberté's choice of attire, so viewers showered (weather joke) the station with complaints like...

"Weather girl looks like she never went home from last night's stripper gig."

I assume the complainer, whose message arrived on a rolled-up scroll sealed with wax, was referring to the strip club chain Mostly Covered—where you can see the sexiest necks on the Sunset Strip! Full of well-behaved men politely saying, "Take off your blazer, please!" But he wasn't alone. The station received so many complaints, in real time, over Facebook and email, that someone offscreen handed Liberté a sweater, which she put on and said, "I look like a librarian now." I'm on Liberté's side, but there's no need to disparage the looks of librarians. Although they often dress in muted tones and cozy sweaters, I once saw an unassuming late-forties librarian in Portland break up a fight between two very hearty homeless men in the fiction section. So "looking like a librarian" is a hard-core compliment.

Liberté is easy to defend. She was unfairly attacked and seems like a chipper, smart lady who spells her name in a way that's showy yet charming. But being a good feminist means I have to defend women when they are being treated unfairly no matter who they are.

Megyn Kelly—yes, we're doing this, buckle your fucking seatbelt please—was covering the 2016 Republican National Convention, aka the RNC, aka Clint Eastwood's whiskey-fueled fever dream, aka Racist Coachella, aka White Privilege–palooza, aka the Bigot Easy, while wearing a Ralph Lauren spaghetti-strap top. Just to set the scene, it's Cleveland, Ohio, late July, and inside a closed arena where thousands of angry conservatives are frantically searching for black people to kick out, which creates a lot of body heat, so I can't imagine wearing a fur coat, à la Nancy Reagan, would have been a comfortable choice for Megyn. When I went to the 2012 DNC, in Charlotte, North Carolina, in September to direct videos for Funny or Die, every moment felt like standing inside a bonfire. So Megyn Kelly was wearing this temperature-appropriate strappy number and the Fox News fans were not having it.

They took to their dens, plugged in their computers, dialed up, screamed at their wives to get off the fax, waited till the line was clear, dialed up again, logged into AOL, and then shot off scathing hate emails to Kelly. They called her a whore and wrote that she looked like she was "waiting for a drink at a hotel bar." SICK BURN, person still holding a grudge against the woman at the Holiday Inn Express in Kalamazoo who rejected his offer of sample-size Jim Beam after he told her he'd been keeping it nice and warm next to his crotch. It's an especially unfair bashing of a woman who, under the directives of Rotten Sausage Boner Roger Ailes, sat under a clear desk so those very same Prilosec abusers could stare at her bare, oiled-up legs. Does Megyn Kelly deserve to be judged for the Niagara Falls amount of elitist, white exceptionalist rhetoric that has fallen from her lips? Yes. Does she deserve to be berated because she used the term *reverse racism*? Yes. Does she deserve to be crucified because she refuses to spell her first name properly? Absolutely! But no woman, no matter how terrible, despicable, and hypocritical, deserves to be called a whore for what she's wearing.

It would stand to reason that female reporters in cold climates could kick up their L.L.Bean duck boots and rest easy, knowing they would never have to suffer the same indignities as their sweltering colleagues. But then came Dan Salamone of WFLD in Chicago to prove to everyone, no matter the weather, female wardrobes can't escape the male gaze.

Dan's the executive producer of *Good Day Chicago*, and during an internal meeting, he told female field reporters unless it's "20 degrees or below," they were not allowed to wear hats outside. Why? Because women "look better without [them]." You know, Dan may have a point. Screw surviving the devil winds whipping over Lake Michigan; women *do* look better when there's not a warm winter hat casting a shadow over their fuckholes. Plus, all that face-obscuring fabric makes it impossible for men to understand us.

"Why I not see fuckhole? Me not know what fuckhole is saying!"

The nerve to tell a woman she can't wear a hat in the winter. I lived in Chicago for one year. My downstairs neighbor, Terry Gatzke, described the Chicago winter to me, a person from Texas, as "being hit in the face with a shovel." He wasn't wrong. In October, I was already wearing a full-length down coat while Chicagoans were in light jackets. By the time winter hit, my morning walk from the Monroe Street L stop, to my receptionist job at a snobby French salon, was just me sputtering "FUCK, FUCK, FUCK" until I got inside. I had to let the water run for AN HOUR before it would get hot enough for the assistants to shampoo hair. Chicago winter is no fucking joke.

Then there's Minneapolis's KARE 11 news anchor Jana Shortal, who wrote a story in the Minneapolis *Star Tribune* about breaking TV reporter conventions and fighting to wear jeans and a blazer—a style I call "the Casual Authority." It's a look that says, "We can talk about Turkish political corruption or eat fish and chips. I'm ready for both." It was cool of the *Star Tribune* to publish her piece, but the same paper also published an op-ed in "The Dish by CJ"—a name that's a lot to unpack. The first part of her name is what she does—dish—and the last part are the anonymous letters she hides behind while she spews superficial judgment to Minneapolis locals. She's a Hedda Hopper wannabe and *Star* contributor who used her precious time to criticize Jana for wearing skinny jeans while reporting on the kidnapping and killing of a young boy. In addition to the article, CJ tweeted, "Do you wish you'd worn different jeans/pants @janashortal on Tuesday's Breaking the News which dealt mostly with Jacob Wetterling's death?" CJ, I don't want to go back to the days of pantyhose and skirts for anyone. Pantyhose make my butt itch, the toe seams dig into the space between my toenails and my toes and create an unholy numbing pain, and no one should have the added problem of wardrobe pain when they're delivering horrendous news to whoever still watches the news.

It may seem like America is a uniquely misogynistic country whose hate is focused on female news anchors. But across the pond, things aren't much better. BBC anchor Fiona Bruce suffered a foot injury in 2016, so she thought, "I'll just deliver the 10 o'clock news in these comfy trainers, I will I will." WRONG MOVE, YOU DAFT BIRD! In London, you shove your broken foot into a dress shoe or get ready to hear restrained, passive aggressive critiques!

I remember when @BBCNEWS at 10 was classy. Now it looks like Fiona Bruce was interrupted cleaning out her shed.

Translated into American English, this comment reads, "You fucking cunt! Get your lyfe right, you stupid whore bag!!" Fiona was inundated with this kind of criticism, probably from the people who also voted to Brexit.

Apparently Britain has a thing against comfortable

shoes, which is not at all surprising for a country that divides its classes by whether or not they live upstairs or downstairs. Nicola Thorp was working as a temp at Price Waterhouse Cooper in London, when she was told to go home and change from flats to heels. When Thorp pointed out the obvious sexism in requiring women to wear toe-murdering footwear but not men, her FEMALE supervisor dropped some supreme knowledge on her. "Men aren't used to wearing heels." Excellent point, dummy. Here's a fun history lesson for everyone: Male ninth-century Persian horseback riders invented heels. Which makes sense: It's a shoe that says "I don't need to walk. I ride an expensive animal. To prove to you how rich I am, I will put things on my feet to make walking impossible." Man heels were used to keep feet stable in stirrups so real men could murder things with their bows and arrows. In other words, heels began as a specialty sporting shoe. Requiring women to wear heels at their job now is like if in five hundred years women were made to wear skis to work. "Alison, I don't care if you can't walk up stairs or fit in elevators, you wear skis to work or you're fired."

Heels were such a symbol of masculinity, they were adopted by European aristocratic men, and it wasn't until the seventeenth century that upper-echelon women started wearing them. So it makes sense that everyone in the world associates heels with sophistication and class, even though they were trendy during a century when people wore perfume so they wouldn't vomit at the smell of their own Baroque BO.

Not to brag, but I can wear a low heel—under 2.5 inches—for almost forty-five entire minutes before I need to pry them off, jaws-of-life style, and stretch out my cramping, throbbing feet. One time I stupidly wore heels out in Brooklyn. It was 2002, when the cool bars and restaurants were very far apart—thank you, I *am* constantly ahead of trends—and there were no cabs, so I spent the last hour of my night walking barefoot in the soupy, rotten-food-smelling, oil-slicked streets of Red Hook looking for a secret speakeasy never to be found. It took three days to get the asphalt out of my toenails.

So I can't begin to imagine what it's like waiting tables in heels. But Cheryl Haase can. She's a fifty-two-year-old waitress at Foxwoods Resort Casino in Connecticut, and had to SUE for the right to wear flats. The casino would only let their waitresses wear normal, earthbound shoes if they had a doctor's note, and if after a year, they were still unable to force a stiletto to their broken feet, they were unceremoniously fired or forced to take another position. If you were unable to balance yourself on wobbly foot stilts, you would leave Foxwoods no choice but to remove you from your job, and it would be 100 percent your fault. Cheryl decided to sue management for their obvious sexism. She said this about her decision: "Most of us girls have been here for 20 years...this job has really done a number on our feet and they know it." The casino is owned by the Mashantucket Pequot tribe, so—in a way—I get it. We stole your land, diseased your people into extinction, and we assumed you'd accept Kevin Costner as one of your own. But please, don't take revenge on cocktail waitresses' feet.

And it's not just women working at bars who need doctor's notes in order to wear flats; it's even female barflys. In Riverside, California, there's a bar called ProAbition, and yes, I spelled that correctly. A promoter for the bar posted an advertisement that read "Ladies: No flat shoes or sandals. Must have heels. Exception will be made if injured." I want to see what happens when you walk into a podiatrist's office and ask, "Can you write me a note so I can wear flats to a flapper bar and get wasted on gin rickeys?"

I hope this podiatrist (a woman, in case your brain is sexist) says, "First of all, don't believe the hype— the '20s fucking sucked. Poverty, rise of the KKK, no *Bachelor in Paradise*."[2] Then I hope the good doctor

---

2   The only reality show I respect because everyone is very honest about just being there to fuck on a beach.

explains to you what repeated wearing of heels does to your body. "They trap your back nerves, fuck with your center of gravity, damage your Achilles, give you corns, hammertoes, stress fractures, and pump bump, which is when you get a permanent lump on the back of your foot. Your feet get hunchbacked, which means they're not good for walking anymore; they're only good for ringing church bells. And when you see an old lady scooting around town in heels, know that she has to, because her calf muscles and tendons are so damaged from foot torture all her life it hurts to be flat footed."

Ladies, if anyone forces you to wear heels, you look them in the eyes and say, "Heels are bad for my neck, my back, my pussy, and my crack."

We've been talking about situations where women have been barred from wearing "inappropriate" (i.e., comfortable) clothes in formal settings: tank tops and skinny jeans on news shows, flats in bars. But what about when there's no question what you're wearing is exactly the perfect outfit for the occasion? It happened in Canada to a woman working out at her gym—and, honestly, when things go wrong in Canada, it makes me panic. Where am I supposed to go when America starts selling guns at Taco Bell? Jenna Vecchio was working out at her local gym when she was told by a "gym supervisor" her tank top was too small for her chest and was asked to cover up. She was wearing a regular, belly-covering, cleavage-encasing tank top. According to her post about the incident, her workout shirt was "no different than many other women's tank tops at the club." When Jenna pointed this out to management, the gym supervisors said it didn't matter what other women were wearing and "due to my chest size I could not wear a tank top."

Here's how I know this is sexism at its ugliest. There's a guy at my gym who wears a tank top that looks like it was attacked by flying scissors. It's like the *Les Mis* flag of tank tops. I have seen his nipples more times than my husband's and not *once* has gym staff walked up to him and said, "Sir, could you cover your teacup-sized 'roid nips?"

It might seem like I've already shared a ton of examples—but, like Megyn Kelly's shoulders, shit's barely being covered here. This issue is cancerous and I haven't even gotten to the yoga pant: a genre of legging widely reviled for its tight fit, which reveals an actual human woman is wearing them. This pant has gotten girls sent home from school, women kicked off United flights and body-shamed by online man gangs, and has served as inspiration for online fat-shaming festivals. You know, where men in ketchup-stained *Short Circuit 2* shirts network a bunch of computers together in a warehouse and attack a woman for no reason other than they don't have a healthy outlet for their rage. Montana representative David Moore tried to expand the state's decency laws to include yoga pants because they "should be illegal in public anyway." Desert Ridge High School in Arizona even blamed the future unemployment of high school boys on the domino effect that occurs when boy sees young woman in yoga pants, boy gets distracted, boy fails all his classes, boy works as a fry cook. Boys getting distracted is not the female student's problem. I spent half my time in high school looking into basketball shorts to stare at dicks and I graduated with a 4.0. Sounds like these boys have a time-management problem, not a yoga pant problem.

It's so overwhelming and I'm not even done! *Discovery Girls* magazine tells eight-year-old girls what bathing suit is best suited for her body type. A Dillard's sales clerk tells a teenager to wear Spanx under her prom dress. The Chicago Bar Association puts on an ENTIRE FASHION SHOW to illustrate to recent female legal grads how not to dress—including no ponytails or flashy wedding rings, you braggy bitches. What can you do as a woman to avoid this constant attack on the way you choose to look? A head-to-toe cover? Ask any Muslim woman how that goes over. Especially at French beaches.[3] Not well.

---

3   Google it.

These are women presented with stupid obstacles to personal clothing choice because everyone else thinks it's their right to weigh in on the matter. If you need an illustration, see how many times people comment on your appearance in a day. Maybe you put on a striped T-shirt and walk to coffee in the morning and the barista says, "I like your shirt." And you're feeling good about yourself but then you go to your mailbox store and the woman behind the desk comments, "My granddaughter has a shirt like that. Is it a children's shirt?" and you know she's being a bitch but she has nerve damage in her left leg, so you let it go. And then you meet your friend for lunch and she says, "Your shirt is great but I feel like it would look better on someone with bigger boobs," and you think, "DO YOU EVEN LIKE ME?!?" So you walk home, grab your terrier mix, and hold his cute face and challenge him to love you despite your polarizing cotton tee. And you know what your dog does? He licks your face. And you know why women love dogs? Because they don't talk about our fucking shirts.[4]

We can combat this appearance-fueled shame fest by starting with ourselves. We have to stop criticizing how women dress. So when you're watching

---

4   And if you find a dog that talks, kill it. He will have strong opinions on whether or not you can pull off bell sleeves.

your friend Kalisa, who went to get everyone nachos, walking back to your seats, and you start talking shit with Mila about how Kalisa doesn't look good in an A-line skirt and it's not the right thing to wear to a baseball game, is she trying to get fucked today, 'cause you thought you were there to look at butts and get day drunk, stop yourself. Recognize you're part of the problem, and acknowledge to Mila that it doesn't matter what Kalisa is wearing in case that bitch was cranked to double down. When Kalisa sits down, you grab her chin, look her in the eye, and say, "You is smart, you is kind, you is important." Because it's been a long time since she's heard it.

EVERYONE HAS A CHOICE...
UNLESS YOU'RE A WOMAN AND
IT'S BEEN TAKEN AWAY FROM YOU

Abortion has been legal since *Roe v. Wade* was decided in 1973, and ever since then, America's religious zealots have been trying to find ways to Make Abortion Illegal Again. These politically powerful life crusaders pine for the good old days when scared women without an alternative shoved hangers up their vaginas, drank turpentine, opium, poisonous tea, or grain fungus, and let leeches loose in their uterus to end unwanted pregnancies.

What to make of these morally superior men who are absolutely OBSESSED with the choices women make with their bodies? Yes, we know they're mostly white, very straight, wear ill-fitting suit pants that balloon at the bottom like fancy Russian curtains, and smile when they say terrible things like, "God sent Katrina to punish the gay-loving Gulf Coast."

Erin Gibson

They'd probably describe *Footloose* as an '80s movie where Kevin Bacon attacks religious freedom. Unfortunately for half the population, their campaign to end abortion access in the United States has been ridiculously successful. In the late '70s, nearly three thousand doctors performed abortions. Now the number is almost half. In 1978, Kentucky had seventeen abortion providers. As of 2017, they are down to one for the entire state.

These clinics are crumbling under Targeted Restrictions of Abortion Providers—also known by the cruelly ironic acronym, TRAP—laws, which really do TRAP abortion providers in a quicksand of unnecessary regulations. It's a brilliant scheme cooked up by conservatives to bog clinics down with expensive regulations so they're forced to close. Abortion is still legal; it's just not available. It's political magic that would make Criss Angel[1] wonder, "How do they do it?!"

It's all possible thanks to 1992's *Planned Parenthood v. Casey*, which allowed individual states the right to regulate abortions... as long as the regulation did not

---

1 Some fun things I know about Criss Angel: (1) His Las Vegas estate has a garden called "Whimsical Way" where eerie statues of children play along the path. (2) His pool was named one of the Top Five most beautiful residential pools by the Association of Pool & Spa Professionals. (3) According to my friend April, he ends his Vegas show with the words "Follow me on Twitter."

pose an "undue burden" on a woman's right to an abortion.

Allowing states to set the rules on abortion as long as they don't create obstacles is like my mom telling me on my sixteenth birthday I could take her Ford Escort for a joyride as long as I was careful. Mom, the first thing I did was run three red lights; the last thing I did was nearly flip the car by taking a HARD right turn, and I was laughing the whole time because I thought tempting fate was fun. How could you be so naive?

TRAP laws are a full *Phantom of the Opera* scenario. The laws go by sensible names like the Abortion Patients Enhanced Safety Act to make them seem like medical protections, but underneath the mask and cape, they're just nasty legislative obstacles like:

- Mandating the facility's hallway width be ridiculously large (for the gurneys women don't need).
- Requiring emergency room admitting privileges for abortion doctors—a high bar for them to clear, because you know who wants less to do with abortion doctors than anti-choicers? Emergency rooms. Especially those affiliated with a Catholic medical association whose religious beliefs conflict with accepted standards of reproductive care.

- Waiting periods, which can make a $400 to $1,000 abortion cost a lot more, forcing women to drive hundreds of miles for a procedure and oftentimes spend the night while they wait—up to two days in some states!—for their procedure to be approved. You can get a gun faster than you can an abortion in the United States. Women are better off strapping a deer head to their pelvis and walking into the woods to let a hunter take care of the problem.
- Forced ultrasounds—where they narrate what's going on in your uterus, which I would agree to if David Attenborough voiced it.
- Mandating that doctors use scare tactics on women considering abortions, like telling them they could become infertile, depressed, or even suicidal from the procedure.
- Making fetus funerals mandatory, such as in Texas, where fetuses had to be buried or cremated, rather than be disposed of with other medical waste like tumors or liposuction goo. The woman undergoing the abortion or miscarriage had to pony up the money. A federal court blocked it. Oh, and Mike Pence's famous fetus funeral bill also got blocked. The bill was put together so badly that the language dictated burying period blood as well, since around half of miscarriages happen shortly after a fertilized egg

is implanted and occur at roughly the same time a woman would expect her period. A woman could have a miscarriage and not know it, then be fined for not burying her uterine lining. Which I do anyway, as part of the curse-casting ritual I perform with my coven, Witches Be Crazy.

All these "protective" measures are about as medically necessary as my nose job. Which I had because I, um, got hit in the face with a basketball (or another reason it's clearly a lie). This won't shock you, but doctors don't like TRAP laws. They're opposed by the American College of Obstetricians & Gynecologists and the American Medical Association for being based on Christian control tactics and not medical science. But states keep passing them, y'all, 'cause like 1998 Courtney Love, anti-choicers do not GIVE. A. FUCK.

According to the Guttmacher Institute, my favorite reproductive health research organization and a name that's fun to say with a mouth full of French onion soup, the stats on abortion restrictions are terrifying. From 1980 to 2010, the control-of-female-bodies-measures introduced per year hovered around twenty to thirty. In 2010, they jumped to nearly ninety and are staying strong. Most of them were enacted by North Dakota, North Carolina,

Arkansas, and Texas—the One Direction of anti-choice states.

In order to get the full picture of what this state-level rights rollback looks like, let's see what Texas, my home state, is tryin' to get away with.

Texas is called the Lone Star State for a reason—it's their rating on Yelp. It's a state filled with hateful religious conservatives, people I know well because they were the parents who bullied me in high school. They're relatively harmless when they're blaming you for their daughter Kristy's smoking habit when it was Kristy who gave you your first cigarette and you fucking know it, Ms. Dowdy! But then they run for office and start ruining a lot of people's lives at once. Three of the finest examples of what I'm talking about are Reps Glenn Hegar, Harvey Hilderbran, and Jodie Anne Laubenberg—the Charlie's Angels of anti-choice Texas legislators. In 2013, they authored TRAP bill SB5, a grab bag of abortion regulations essentially shutting down most abortion clinics in Texas. Jodie made a name for herself nationally by showing Americans that despite her ability to regulate abortion, she does not understand it. When responding to an exemption to this bill, proposed by a Democrat, for rape victims to be able to get an abortion after the proposed twenty-week limit, Jodie took her expertise as a nonmedical professional[2] and NRA shill and attempted to answer a question she was not at all qualified to respond to. She said rape victims don't need exemptions because their rape kits cause abortions and a "woman can get cleaned out, basically a D&C." A D&C is not an all-women's fantasy role-playing game; it stands for dilation and curettage—a procedure doctors perform after a miscarriage to remove the extra stuff left behind that could cause infection or bleeding. PolitiFact contacted Laubenberg to ask her to please explain, and she told them she "knows a rape kit doesn't involve D&C." What she meant to say was, "After being wrong, and publicly called out for it, I have learned that what I said was stupid, and now I'm pretending I knew it the whole time." She tried to backtrack and claimed what she was trying to say was rape victims might have the opportunity to take the morning-after pill but also admitted she knew that was not rape kit protocol. I don't accept Jodie's rape kit ignorance in a time when every human in America has seen one episode of Dick Wolf's rape crime porn *Law & Order: SVU*. An episode is always guaranteed to be

---

2   Her Wikipedia lists her as co-owner of a business called CompuHelp Services, which LinkedIn says has forty employees. When I typed the business address into Google Maps, I see a tract home, which seems fishyyyyyy. Also, one of the few on the block without a pool.

on no matter the time or channel. I've spent more time accidentally bingeing *Law & Order: SVU* than I have purposely watching shows I actually like. I can tell you what the entire episode is about from just watching the cold open and it's not a skill I am proud of. But based on my *LO: SVU* knowledge alone, I would be a better candidate than Jodie Anne to represent the interests of the women of Texas. Gung gung.[3]

Jodie and her BFFs Glenn and Harvey got to work getting SB5 approved like three screaming skulls on fire...until the saloon doors to the Texas state legislature swung open and Wendy Davis came power walking down the aisle in her Mizuno Women's Wave Rider sneakers. She fastened her back brace; adjusted her catheter, which she had inserted so she could pee without leaving the floor; and filibustered the bill for the next eleven hours.[4] Unlike Jodie Anne Lodedturd, Wendy knows a thing or two about reproductive rights. During her second marriage, she had two abortions due to medical issues with the fetuses, and she wasn't letting Texas get away with this bill without a bar fight.

I was in Minneapolis the day she filibustered,

---

3   That's the *Law & Order* sound effect. Also called "doink doink."
4   The filibuster is impressive, yeah sure, but having had a catheter removed, I will tell you, was the real pain she suffered. Taking it out feels like having an old rusted rake pulled through your urethra.

there to do a live show for my podcast, *Throwing Shade.* We'd been to a bunch of cities already, and I was tired from late shows, beer, and airplane small talk,[5] but when I saw what Wendy was doing, I stayed up all night to watch her and my pro-choice shit-kicking sisters fill up the state capital. I wished I was there, rabble-rousing with my Southern sisters, screaming at old men in Stetson hats who reek of slow-cooked brisket and sexism. Getting thrown out of the capital, then going to Chuy's and overfilling my stomach with their super yumyum queso. But I was in Minneapolis, so I protested alone, then picked at some juniper-spiced meatballs that did not pack the same gut rot as the delicious stomach punch that is melted cheese, chiles, and salty-ass chips.

It seemed like Wendy's efforts worked. Her filibuster successfully delayed the passage of SB5. Then Governor Rick Perry got involved when the bill was reintroduced in a second legislative session. On July

---

5   It's particularly exhausting because I am not honest when people ask me what I do and so I have to think of a bunch of lies about being in accounts payable. I used to be a bookkeeper for my step-dad's company, so I know enough to throw someone off my trail, but then at a certain point they wonder why a white business professional is wearing a 1970s T-shirt with horses on it and reading the Malcolm X autobiography, but that's when I put my headphones on. The big ones that say, "I'm done talking forever."

18, 2013, Rick Perry got out of his Yosemite Sam sleeping bag, grabbed his favorite Silly Scents crayon, and signed SB5 into law.

Like MRSA in an Imagine Dragons tour bus, SB5 quickly infected Texas abortion clinics, forcing them to shut down. Twenty-nine of the forty clinics were gone. Women had to drive farther for abortion services and wait times increased. The only way for those remaining clinics to serve the 5.4 million women of reproductive age in Texas would be to develop some sort of lazy Susan with stirrups, and I bet women would be more than happy to be treated like a pepper mill if that meant having access to abortion care.

The case moved up the court system until it reached the Supreme Court in 2016. They ruled in *Whole Woman's Health* (good people) *v. Hellerstedt* (terrible people) that SB5 created an undue burden on women seeking abortions, which is illegal under the 1992 verdict of *Planned Parenthood v. Casey*. It was a triumph for pro-choicers, but this ruling will not stop any state committed to making abortion disappear. Trying to stop anti-choicers is like fighting vampires by tripping them as they walk by. Governor Greg Abbott,[6] the anti-Muslim voter ID–loving oil

---

6   Abbott went on Glenn Beck's radio show to respond to the NFL threatening to not come back to Texas if they pass bathroom

dick who replaced Rick Perry, said in response to the Supreme Court ruling, "Texas will continue to fight for higher-quality healthcare standards for women while protecting our most vulnerable—the unborn."

Governor Abbott is a hero to the unborn, but once the baby's out of the womb, he and other politicians like him get a case of "pro-life amnesia." According to the Center for Public Policy Priorities 2016 State of Texas Children report, one in four children in Texas lives in poverty, with 19 percent of them living in "high poverty." I don't hear Greg "Life Is Beautiful" Abbott talking about how he can make the lives of children in his state better. He'll spend over half a million dollars defending medically unsound abortion restrictions but not helping single moms get housing, jobs, and child care.

Step into the pro-life world, children…and suffer.

Arkansas came up with a monstrous fever dream of a bill to let a husband sue a doctor to stop his wife from getting a second-trimester abortion, with no exception for spousal rape. According to the smar-

---

bills. The governor said, "I gotta tell you, I cannot name, or even count, the number of Texans who told me that they were not watching the NFL—they were protesting the NFL this year—because of the gross political statement allowed to be made by the NFL." Bitch, please, what a liar. Texas couldn't quit football if they tried. You take football out of Texas and all you have is a bunch of straight guys mumbling to themselves on a park bench like Cate Blanchett in *Blue Jasmine*.

ties at Guttmacher, 10 percent of women seeking abortions have second-trimester abortions. There are a lot of reasons women wait to have second-trimester abortions—scrounging up the extra money to get an abortion, fetal health concerns, or sometimes women with erratic periods might not know they're pregnant. America's made enough TV shows about women going to take a shit and then surprise, it wasn't a pastrami sandwich, it was a baby, so I think we can all get on board with the idea that women might not always be in tune with what is happening in our confusing bodies. Whatever the reason women get second-trimester abortions, Guttmacher agrees that removing barriers to first-trimester abortions would make second-trimester abortions less necessary, especially among black women and undereducated women. You would think that Arkansas, the fifth-poorest state in America (according to their own Department of Health), would tackle their shameful and embarrassing health care problems—short life expectancy, high infant mortality, and low health literacy—as outlined by their own State Health Assessment and Improvement Plan.

Oklahoma, a firework stand shaped like a state, pushed HB 1441, introduced by Justin Humphrey, a guy who looks like he's moderating a panel at Cormac McCarthyCon—cowboy hat, rimless glasses, and an unshakable love of the bolo tie. His bill would require the written consent of the fetus's father before a woman would be allowed to have an abortion. Here's Humphrey's inspiration for the bill:

I believe one of the breakdowns in society is that we've excluded the man out of all types of these decisions.

I have a very long slide show for Justin Humphrey. It contains photo after photo of panels and policy hearings on reproductive rights on the state and national level involving zero women. Forever since always, men have been taking massive amounts of time from their golf games and prayer circles to mandate what kind of reproductive rights women are allowed to have. I would LOVE to live in the world Justin *thinks* we're living in, where women are calling all the shots and guys like Justin have nuthin' to do but keep their traps shut and shuffle around in their ostrich-skin boots lookin' for a fine piece o' pine to whittle into a boat.

I prefer that world to this one, where Justin is emboldened to spew his retrograde philosophies. Philosophies like "I understand that they [women] feel like that is their body. I feel like it is a separate— what I call them is, you're a 'host.'"[7]

---

7 Some hero went on Justin's Wikipedia page and changed the words *mother* and *wife* to "host."

Justin, sorry, but as a host, if a guest comes uninvited, they're not welcome. I can't allow it. Not only is it rude, but there also won't be enough prosciutto-wrapped asparagus for the guests who actually were invited. But Justin not only demands I host the unwanted guest, but thinks I'm also to blame for not planning for its possible appearance. Justin explains:

> …and you know when you enter into a relationship you're going to be that host and so, you know, if you pre-know that then take all precautions and don't get pregnant.

But sometimes you don't "pre-know" you're gonna be a host. Sometimes you're working in Seattle for a week and you meet a sinew-y Adonis in Ashtanga class who can warrior two like a motherfucking champion. It's getting hot—and not just because you're flowing in a 100-degree room. After class, he says hi and asks if you'd like to "namastay for a tea." You get he's being unfunny on purpose. Over a pot of sencha, he tells you about his mother's struggle with Crohn's. What?! Your sister has Crohn's! When he talks, he touches your hand, your leg, your shoulder.

Next thing you know, you two are fucking like coked-up dolphins in your Airbnb. Tits on the windows, bent over a Turkish fireplace chair, in the sheets, on the floor, everywhere. You take a break to gulp some water, and as you stand up, a gooey condom rolls down your leg. How long was it off? Who knows? The point is, you can pre-know until the fucking cows come home, but that doesn't mean condoms don't slip off when you're fucking a stranger on a work trip.

Justin was justifiably hammered by critics for his dumb statements. But the sad news is, guys like Justin, they rarely learn anything when they screw up. They justify. Justin told reporters in the aftermath, "When I use the term host, it's not meant to degrade women. I actually went and Googled that. I went to Webster, and I couldn't find a better term." You stopped too soon, Justin! You were in the H's! A few pages later you would've found the word *human*. At this point I'm wondering what Justin *does* know. Does he know the bright circle in the sky is the sun or does he think it's God's belly button?

The sad news is, it's not just Republicans who want to see abortion outlawed. There are Democrats who are anti-choice, despite being members of a party whose official website clearly states that women have a "right to a safe and legal abortion" and members of the party will fight all "laws and policies that impede a woman's access to abortion."

Senator Joe Donnelly from Indiana, picking an

awful way to reach across the aisle, said this about including other Democratic anti-choice politicians, like himself, in the party:

> We ought to be able to include everyone, as opposed to saying "no, we don't want these folks, even though they fight with us on jobs, even though they fight with us for economic rights, even though they fight with us on healthcare."

No, Joe. That's not what we should do. Abortion is legal and being a politician means representing the interests of constituents, which include women. We can't start carving out special little excuses for our stupid personal beliefs that hurt women. I personally believe there shouldn't be more than five Nikola Tesla experts in an episode of *Ancient Aliens*, but I would never disrupt the delicate lives of divorced dads who love to drone on about aliens giving Tesla the plans for the Internet in 1926.

Former Michigan Democratic representative Bart Stupak, the kind of classic Midwestern man who I picture spending his Saturdays in a wood-paneled basement dusting collectible beer steins, nearly tanked the ACA because he wanted anti-abortion provisions.

These Democrats and Republicans (and British Nationals, Democratic Unionist, National Front, Fianna Fáil, Sinn Féin, Social Encounter Party, Family First, Democratic Labour Party, Workers' Party, etc.) all legislate and talk like women *want* to get abortions. Like it's a day at the spa. "I can't decide if I want to have the pregnancy tissue removed before or after my oxygen facial." Abortions, for many of us, are a necessary part of reproductive care. Not everyone wants to be a mom, and even if we do, for a lot of women, having a child is a question of economics. My besties at Guttmacher reported that abortion rates are high during recessions, particularly among low-income women. And for the women who can't afford an abortion, they are three times more likely to dip into poverty while they're raising a toddler and struggling to find steady employment. A single mom making less than $59,000 (the average income for a single mother is $26,000—so all of them) will spend nearly $11,453 per child per year. That's a fifth to a half of her income, and welfare reforms make it harder and harder for working moms to get the assistance they need from their "pro-life" states. Pack all that on top of the fact that kids are fucking nihilists, they bite, they pull hair, they're small little terrorists who will not stop demanding you pretend to lick their foot like an ice cream cone even though you put on *Daniel Tiger's Neighborhood*, thinking they'll zombie out long enough for you to suck down half a cup of cold coffee. Oh, and give up your dreams of putting on something other than pajamas today. You won't have time. Add all that to the crushing weight of poverty and you have a life I don't want anyone to have. I want women to have choices. If they get pregnant in high school, like my mother, they should have the option to abort and pursue a fine art career. My mom looks like our teenage babysitter in all my childhood pictures. She was angry and I understand it wasn't just because '80s tops made her look bulky. She traded her freedom for motherhood and a string of unstable, low-paying jobs. Anti-choicers would point to my life as the reason why abortion should be illegal. If my mom aborted me, I wouldn't be able to eat marijuana gummies at the Tim Burton LACMA exhibit or roll my windows down and sing every lyric to the karaoke version of "We Didn't Start the Fire" to brag to other LA drivers that I know all the words. My life is great, but this argument that I wouldn't be able to enjoy these things if my mom aborted me is dumb logic, made by people who think they understand how time works because they've seen *Back to the Future*. If my mom aborted me, I would never exist. And not existing means I wouldn't have memories and so I wouldn't miss my life because it never happened.

My allegiance lies with the women who already exist and what they lose when the government takes away their ability to make decisions in their own best interest. I wonder about the drug-induced art my talented mom could have created had she not spent her energy raising kids she wasn't ready for. I wonder what my maternal grandmother would have accomplished without 11 children to worry about. I wonder what marvelous things my paternal grandmother could have done had she not been spending months in the '50s begging landlords to rent an apartment to a single woman with a five-year-old. I come from a long line of women without choices, women who survived insurmountable odds after finding themselves pregnant at a young age without access to birth control or abortion.

For all of them, and the futures they lost, I am a loud, unapologetic abortion champion. In fact, that's my superhero name: Abortion Champion. My costume is flattering and understated, with the symbol of a woman resting easy on my chest. I'm working on an on-theme car wrap, but it takes a long time to get them printed, so in the meantime, I've got sick decals for my Rollerblades. Keep an eye out for me blading toward justice. You'll know it's me 'cause I don't know how to brake, so I have to stop in the grass.

CONCLUSION

Well, that's it. Can you believe we covered so much and still didn't get to INCELS, middle school period bathroom breaks, the struggles of trans women, pregnant detainees, Hollywood being surprised *First Wives Club* was a hit, sexism in China, the corporatization of International Women's Day, eating disorders, child marriage in America, GOP sex scandals, obstacles for female attorneys and the problem with gendering jobs in the first place, Hollywood being surprised *Bridesmaids* was a hit, sexual assault in the Olympics, female artificial intelligence, reproductive care on campus, female incarceration, bikini season, workplace discrimination against mothers, imposter syndrome, loan discrimination, Hollywood being surprised *Girls Trip* was a hit, vocal fry, One Million Moms, and when the FUCK is Harriet Tubman gonna show up on my twenty-dollar bills?!

I'm sure some of you now think I'm some sort of anti-male misandrist nightmare, but nothing could be further from the truth. It's very hard to make jokes and rip into good guys doing the right thing, which is why Mark Ruffalo and my husband are barely mentioned. Fingers crossed Mark Ruffalo doesn't let us down between now and press time. Or, Jesus, *after* press time. I'm lucky to be surrounded by a ton of straight men who, unlike Angela Merkel, the world's most powerful woman, have no problem calling themselves "feminists." Men who are willing to back up the label with pro-women actions and words, and correct other guys who haven't gotten the memo.

The world is a really frightening place right now, but I truly believe what we are experiencing is the death rattle of powerful toxic masculinity. We're trying to take Laffy Taffy out of a sugar-addicted toddler's powerful hands, and they do not give up chewy sweet things without a temper tantrum. It's going to be hard, and we might get kicked in the face a couple times, and probably bit with teeny nail-like baby teeth, but we will eventually win.

As we battle to topple the patriarchy, we must deal with how the small victories redefine us. What do we look like when the rules are burned to the ground? Some of us are struggling with the new power to be who we are, cautiously dipping our toes into unfamiliar ponds, unsure if it's truly safe to jump in. I can't wait until a trans woman in a polyamorous relationship is the mayor of a small town in Alabama, a black woman is president, and Ted Nugent is illegal. That future can't come fast enough for me, but I recognize that dumping the binary past so quickly is not so easy for some. A lot of people are coming to terms with and erasing the toxic culture that's raised them, a belief system built on unfairness and superiority that subconsciously dictates every interaction. We have to be kind to one another as we stumble through this process. I'm not saying we shouldn't punch Nazis or put Stephen Miller in jail. I'm saying that, for the people who are trying to do better and want to change, we must help them because we need them on our side.

In this world of change, it's important to evaluate our own prejudices. For example, my dislike for the French. I've made it clear in the book how I feel about the country but allow me to explain. The French have betrayed me. For two years in high school, I studied French. I loved the French and I loved speaking French. In my mind, the French culture was intellectually superior and leaving America in the dust with its progressive ideals. So you can imagine how heartbroken I was when I finally got to go to Paris and realized that France has the same sexism, anti-Semitism, homophobia, racism, and ruder store clerks than America. Would I go back and change my criticisms about the French in this book? No way. I've been clear that I think America is an embarrassing place, just like France, and I think it's important to let the French know they're no better than America. A sentence I hope burns through their souls. There's nothing as terrible as being just like America. Still, if a French person came to me, quivering with self-doubt, and said, "Help me end my audacious, detestable attitude that unsuccessfully masks my insecurity," I would take their hand and say, "Bonjour. *Je m'appelle* Erin. Come, mon ami…we will go to la boulangerie and figure out how to usher in a new future together over buttery croissants that your people probably stole from another culture."

All of this is to say, the world does not have to be like this; even the French can change. People want us to be powerless, they want us not to see the oppression that holds us down. All you have to do is see it and change as much of it as you can handle. No one is asking you to change the *world* by yourself, so just start with your world.

ACKNOWLEDGMENTS

Allow me to brag about my family for a moment. My mother is a strong woman with a dark sense of humor who can take criticism (as long as it's couched in a really good joke) and who will nurse any animal she finds on a sidewalk back to health. She is a caretaker, a teacher, a learner, the bullshit police, and makes the best dinner rolls I've ever had in my mouth. My father is one of the smartest people I know, whose passion for the absurd is boundless. As a veteran, he taught me to be regimented and precise, to listen and be kind, and how to bury my cigarette butts in the sand so my tracks can't be traced. My sister will yell at anyone being unkind to a waiter and is unafraid to start shit with any motherfucker doing the wrong thing. Thank you for being yourselves. What we lacked in being a good family we made up for by being good people. Thank you to Steven Blum, Michael Hartney, and April Richardson for putting your eyeballs on these words and giving me your honest opinions on what sucked and what didn't. My manager Jennie Church-Cooper, who, excuse me, Patty Jenkins, is the real

Wonder Woman. We knew each other when we were just figuring things out, and honey, we figured it out. #missvanji To Adam MacLean for somehow flying into my life and not letting me hug you to death with my extreme adoration for every single word that comes out of your mouth. To my strong LA women: Alison Becker, Rachel North, April Richardson, Annie Mebane, Emma Rathbone. Okay, so we're all brunettes, so what? It means nothing! To Hannah Gordon, my book agent, who put so much time into this book to sell it, then left the business to help people who need her passion and warmth. To Adriann Ranta for hopping in there and making the transition smooth, for addressing my neurotic book cover emails with sincerity and calmness, and for being part of what might be the greatest female team ever to be assembled to sell, write, and produce a book. To Suzanne O'Neill, my editor, who I felt SO SORRY for because I wrote this whole thing like a screenplay with choppy sentences and the first draft was not good and you know what? NEVERTHELESS, she supported me and guided me and gave me ENDLESS patience even though I was convinced she would want the advance back. Thank you for being Quincy-Jones-on-Ringo-Starr level honest with me. To Lisa Rivlin the Lawyer, who needs her own TV show, which I am working on without your permission (sue me!). Thank you to Carolyn Kurek for not wanting to murder me for my inability to remember when I should *italicize* and when I should use "quotation marks." Tiffany Sanchez and Jordan Rubinstein, massive thanks to both of you for your embarrassing amounts of creativity and gusto. You hawked this book like Paul Ryan in an *Atlas Shrugged* circle jerk—unrelenting, steadfast, singularly focused. Elece Green, who listened to my voice nonstop for too many days to mold it into a perfectly produced audiobook, you deserve all the awards. Thank you to Ricky Middlesworth for being my cover partner and for making picture taking so much fun. Never stop laughing the way you do; I need it. Melissa Gould McNeely, it's impossible for you to be better at your job, but you manage to outdo yourself every time we work together. Valerie Jackson and Kristina Frisch, how lucky am I that Kimmy Gatewood sent me your way? I'm jealous of the women of *GLOW* for being able to work with you two for more than one day. Thank you to Eleanor Winkler for not only introducing me to breaky, but for being a hands-on, all-or-nothing producer who is always the calmest person in the room. To all the *Throwing Shade* fans, let me make it very clear that your support was integral in getting this book done. #ladyattorney #easterbunny #tittywitch Thank you to my ex-husband, Michael Blieden, for being supportive in weird ways but mostly for being so much cooler as a friend. And then let's talk about my main bros. Bryan Safi, for being the smartest man I've ever had the pleasure of being in business with. Your silliness is the only thing that makes me feel joy these days. I love you like a brother because you are my brother. You are the longest relationship I've ever been in and that should scare you. And a massive overtly sexual thank-you to the person who deserves mountains of praise, my SECOND & BEST husband, Alessandro Minoli. I'm not going to say "I'm nothing without you" because I was a fully formed human when we met, but I love us together. We make a great team, although I wonder how you put up with the nights of me spiraling out of control, the mornings of me spiraling out of control, and the afternoons of me slamming plates into the dishwasher and screaming "I'm not talented!" I think people should separate when writing big pieces like this. But you still want to get naked with me even after all that and seeing how ugly I am when I wear my nightguard. I love you and I love that you get mad when people you like get sent home on *RuPaul's Drag Race*. You're the kindest man I've ever known, and when we can clone people, I think you should volunteer. We need more of you in the world. To Oliver and Micki, who can't read this, but I love you guys. One of you bites strangers and the other one bites my ears, and I can't get enough of any of it. Lastly, thank you to women. You are my sisters.

SOURCES

If you're curious about how I know all this stuff, it's because I read a lot of sad news. But maybe you want to know more about all the depressing things in my book that I (hopefully) made more palatable by couching them in filthy jokes, so here's a list. Arm yourself with patience, your favorite brand of soft-baked chocolate chip cookies (laced with mescaline), and tuck in for a long night of plowing through these comprehensive articles written by (mostly) women who are smarter than me.

INTRODUCTION

Kirsten M. J. Thompson, "A Brief History of Birth Control in the U.S.," www.ourbodiesourselves.org, December 14, 2013.

Lisa Wade, "The Secret Life of Vintage Lysol Douche Ads," www.thesocietypages.org, September 27, 2013.

THE TERRIFYING PROSPECT OF MIKE "VAGINAS ARE THE DEVIL'S MOUTH FLAPS" PENCE

American Medical Association, "Health Care Needs of Lesbian, Gay, Bisexual and Transgender Populations H-160.991," www.policysearch.ama-assn.org, 2017.

American Psychological Association, "American Psychological Association Applauds President Obama's Call to End Use of Therapies Intended to Change Sexual Orientation," www.apa.org, April 9, 2015.

Sources

Miriam Berg, "8 Outrageous Facts About Mike Pence's Record on Reproductive Rights," www.plannedparenthoodaction.org, July 20, 2016.

Emma Green, "White Evangelicals Believe They Face More Discrimination Than Muslims," www.theatlantic.com, March 10, 2017.

Hunter, "Just Another Reminder That Vice President Mike Pence Is Also a Complete Nutcase," www.thedailykos.com, June 19, 2017.

Andrew Kaczynski, "Mike Pence Argued in an Op-Ed That Disney's 'Mulan' Was Liberal Propaganda," www.buzzfeed.com, July 27, 2016.

Jonathan Mahler and Dirk Johnson, "Mike Pence's Journey: Catholic Democrat to Evangelical Republican," www.nytimes.com, July 20, 2016.

Stephen Peters, "Washington Governor Signs Legislation Protecting LGBTQ Youth from Dangerous 'Conversion Therapy,'" www.hrc.org, March 28, 2018.

Megan Twohey, "Mike Pence's Response to H.I.V. Outbreak: Prayer, Then a Change of Heart," www.nytimes.com, August 7, 2016.

HOW TO EXPLAIN #METOO TO THE DUMMIES WHO DON'T GET IT

Ron Dicker, "Ashleigh Banfield Blasts Aziz Ansari Accuser for 'Reckless' Sexual Assault Claim," www.huffingtonpost.com, January 16, 2018.

Caitlin Flanagan, "The Humiliation of Aziz Ansari," www.theatlantic.com, January 14, 2018.

Daphne Merkin, "Publicly, We Say #MeToo. Privately, We Have Misgivings," www.nytimes.com, January 5, 2018.

Tatiana Siegel, "How the #MeToo Movement Could Kill Some Sexy Hollywood Movies," www.hollywoodreporter.com, January 10, 2018.

Various Authors, "Nous défendons une liberté d'importuner, indispensable à la liberté sexuelle," www.lemonde.fr, January 9, 2018.

Suzanne Venker, "#MeToo Isn't About Sexual Harassment, It's About Destroying Masculinity," www.washingtonexaminer.com, January 10, 2018.

Katie Way, "I Went on a Date with Aziz Ansari. It Turned into the Worst Night of My Life," www.babe.net, January 14, 2018.

WATCH OUT FOR THESE FECKLESS CUNTS

Ryan Teague Beckwith, "What You Should Know About Phyllis Schlafly," www.time.com, September 6, 2016.

Steve Benen, "Ellmers Urges Men to Bring Policy 'Down to a Woman's Level,'" www.msnbc.com, July 15, 2014.

Sources

Emily Crockett, "The Lawsuit Accusing Trump of Raping a 13-Year-Old Girl, Explained," www.vox.com, November 5, 2016.

Sarah Ellison, "Inside Ivanka and Tiffany Trump's Complicated Sister Act," www.vanityfair.com, February 2017.

Susan Patton, "A Little Valentine's Day Straight Talk," www.wsj.com, February 13, 2014.

Avi Selk, "A Woman's Bold Campaign Ad Points Out the One Thing She Doesn't Have," www.washingtonpost.com, November 30, 2017.

PERIODS DON'T JUST RUIN PANTIES, THEY RUIN FREEDOM

Emma Court, "New York Is the Latest State to Scrap Tampon Tax," www.marketwatch.com, April 12, 2016.

Olivia Goldhill, "Period Pain Can Be 'Almost As Bad As a Heart Attack.' Why Aren't We Researching How to Treat It?" www.qz.com, February 15, 2016.

Jen Gunter, "Livia Isn't a New Off Switch for Period Pain, It's an Expensive TENS Unit," www.drjengunter.wordpress.com, May 24, 2016.

Matthew Solovey, "Vaginally Administered ED Medication May Alleviate Menstrual Cramping," www.news.psu.edu, December 5, 2013.

BANKRUPTING THE MAKEUP MEN

Loulla-Mae Eleftheriou-Smith, "Revlon CEO Lorenzo Delpani Believes He Can 'Smell' Black People When He Walks into a Room, According to a Legal Claim," www.independent.co.uk, January 2, 2015.

Rachel Krause, "Sally Hansen Is Real—& Way Cooler Than You Imagined," www.refinery.29.com, October 16, 2017.

Aaron Smith, "Revlon Just Got Its First Female CEO in the Company's 86-Year History," www.money.cnn, May 23, 2018.

Gabrielle Solomon, "10 Top-Paid CEOs," www.cnn.com, May 31, 2017.

EMBRACE THE WOMAN YOU ARE, GIRL

Emily St. John Mandel, "The Gone Girl with the Dragon Tattoo on the Train: Why Are There So Many Books with 'Girl' in the Title?" www.fifethirtyeight.com, October 27, 2016.

Bethany McLean, "The Backstory Behind That 'Fearless Girl' Statue on Wall Street," www.theatlantic.com, March 13, 2017.

Sources

PUTTING THE "STEM" BACK IN FEMINISTEM

Robin Abcarian, "Justice for a Sex-Harassing Berkeley Astronomy Professor," www.latimes.com, October 20, 2015.

Catalyst, Stats about women in STEM, www.catalyst.org.

Hannah Devlin, "Tim Hunt Sexism Dispute: UCL Ruling Council Back Decision to Let Him Go," www.theguardian.com, July 9, 2015.

Rachel Feltman, "Sexism in Science: Peer Editor Tells Female Researchers Their Study Needs a Male Author," www.washingtonpost.com, April 30, 2015.

Azeen Ghorayshi, "Here's How Geoff Marcy's Sexual Harassment Went on for Decades," www.buzzfeed.com, November 11, 2015.

Kelly Kasulis, "Here's What We'll Lose with Trump's Proposed NASA Budget Cuts, and Why One Expert Is Calling It Out," www.businessinsider.com, May 24, 2017.

Tyler Kingkade, "A Professor's Sexual Harassment Case Came Out in Congress, and He's Fighting Back," www.buzzfeed.com, May 24, 2017.

Christopher Klein, "Right Stuff, Wrong Gender: The Woman Astronauts Grounded by NASA," www.history.com, July 24, 2017.

Svati Kirsten Narula, "Horrible Advice on Sexual Harassment from an Accomplished Female Scientist," www.qz.com, June 1, 2015.

Bob Sorokanich, "NASA Engineers Offered Sally Ride 100 Tampons for a 7 Day Space Mission," www.gizmodo.com, June 21, 2014.

Talent Innovation, STEM study, www.talentinnovation.org.

Joan C. Williams, Katherine W. Phillips, Erika V. Hall, "Double Jeopardy? Gender Bias Against Women of Color in Science," www.uchastings.edu, 2014.

THE NFL DOES NOT CARE ABOUT YOUR BREAST CANCER

American Cancer Society, "NFL Helps American Cancer Society Fight Breast Cancer," www.cancer.org, October 4, 2016.

CDC, "Breast Cancer Statistics," www.cdc.gov, last updated May 29, 2018.

Maggie Fox, "Breast Cancer Treatments Vary Wildly, Study Finds," www.nbcnews.com, October 10, 2016.

Lea Goldman, "The Big Business of Breast Cancer," www.marieclaire.com, September 14, 2011.

Rebecca R. Ruiz, "4 Cancer Charities Are Accused of Fraud," www.nytimes.com, May 19, 2015.

S. E. Smith, "Pinkification: How Breast Cancer Awareness Got Commodified for Profit," www.theguardian.com, October 3, 2012.

Sources

WRITING A LETTER TO A PERSON YOU DISAGREE WITH TO MAKE THEM SEE HOW WRONG THEY ARE

Amanda Arnold, "Betsy DeVos Sued for Rolling Back Campus Sexual-Assault Protections," www.thecut.com, January 27, 2018.

Association of American Universities, Study on sexual assault, www.aau.edu.

Kelly Faircloth, "Get a Load of Betsy DeVos's Freaking House," www.theslot.com, September 7, 2017.

Lawrence A. Greenfield, "Sex Offense and Offenders: An Analysis of Data on Rape and Sexual Assault," www.bjs.gov, February 1997.

Mikki Kendall, "Why Dress Codes Can't Stop Sexual Assault," washingtonpost.com, April 13, 2016.

Tyler Kinkade, "Texas Tech Investigating Frat for 'No Means Yes, Yes Means Anal' Signs," www.huffingtonpost.com, September 23, 2014.

Heather Murphy, "What Experts Know About Men Who Rape," www.nytimes.com, October 30, 2017.

Sandra Newman, "What Kind of Person Makes False Rape Accusations?" www.qz.com, May 11, 2017.

RAINN, "Victims of Sexual Violence: Statistics," www.rainn.org.

Stephanie Saul and Kate Taylor, "Betsy DeVos Reverses Obama-era on Campus Sexual Assault Investigations," www.nytimes.com, September 22, 2017.

LESBIANS ARE NONE OF OUR BUSINESS

Eric Crowley, "How to Seduce a Lesbian as a Straight Man," www.returnofkings.com, January 9, 2014.

Nicholas DiDomizio, "This Is the Top Porn Search Term of 2015—and Here's What It Can Tell Us," www.mic.com, January 6, 2016.

Sarah Young, "Lesbian Relationships Only Exist Because Men Find It a Turn-On, Claims Study," www.independent.co.uk, June 1, 2017.

STAYING OUT OF MAY/DECEMBER ROMANCES

Kyle Buchanan, "Leading Men Age, but Their Love Interests Don't," www.vulture.com, April 18, 2013.

Mona Chalabi, "What's the Average Age Difference In a Couple?" www.fivethirtyeight.com, January 22, 2015.

Stephen Follows, "Study: How Much Older Are Male Leads in Romantic Films Than Their Female Co-Stars?" www.indiewire.com, June 1, 2015.

Stephen Galloway, "The Woody Allen Interview (Which He Won't Read)," www.hollywoodreporter.com, May 4, 2016.

Sources

Elizabeth Kiefer, "Enraging New Stats About the Age Gap Between Male & Female Romantic Leads," www.refinery29.com, June 1, 2015.

Sandra Song, "Woody Allen Says His Relationship with Wife Soon Yi Is 'Paternal,'" www.papermag.com, July 30, 2015.

LET THE TEENS FUCK EACH OTHER

Emma Gray, "Pam Stenzel, Abstinence-Only Sex Ed Speaker, Reportedly Tells Students 'If You Take Birth Control, Your Mother Probably Hates You,'" www.huffingtonpost.com, April 12, 2013.

Julie F. Kay with Ashley Jackson, "Sex, Lies & Stereotypes: How Abstinence-Only Programs Harm Women and Girls," www.hrp.law.harvard.edu/, 2008.

Andy Kopsa, "Shelly Donahue's Abstinence Education 'WAIT Training,'" www.westword.com, August 11, 2011.

Danielle Paquette, "Why Millennials Have Sex with Fewer Partners Than Their Parents Did," www.washingtonpost.com, May 6, 2015.

Sexuality Information and Education Council of the United States, "A History of Federal Funding for Abstinence-Only-Until-Marriage Programs," www.siecus.org.

Brittanie Shey, "The 6 Creepiest Things About R U Dateable's Justin Lookadoo," www.houstonpress.com, November 14, 2013.

Pam Stenzel, www.pamstenzel.com.

DOCTORS ARE NOT THE BOSS OF YOU

American Heart Association, "Heart Attack Symptoms in Women," www.heart.org, March 30, 2018.

Kai Falkenberg, "While You Were Sleeping," www.marieclaire.com, September 27, 2012.

Tong J. Gan, MB, FRCA, FFARCSI; Peter S. Glass, MB, FFA(SA); Jeff Sigl, PhD; Peter Sebel, MB, BS, PhD, FFARSCI; Fredrick Payne, MD; et al, "Women Emerge from General Anesthesia with Propofol/Alfentanil/Nitrous Oxide Faster than Men," www.anesthesiology.pubs.asahq.org, May 1999.

Philip J. Hilts, "F.D.A. Ends Ban on Women in Drug Testing," www.nytimes.com, March 25, 1993.

Nina Martin and Renee Montagne, "Black Mothers Keep Dying After Giving Birth. Shalon Irving's Story Explains Why," www.npr.org, December 7, 2017.

Susan Morgan, Odile Plaisant, Baptiste Lignier, Bernard J. Moxham,

Sources

"Sexism and Anatomy, as Discerned in Textbooks and as Perceived by Medical Students at Cardiff University and University of Paris Descartes," www.onlinelibrary.wiley.com, June 19, 2013.

Kas Roussy, "Women's Period Seen as Barrier to Medical Research," www.cbc.ca, June 6, 2016.

Mario Testino, "Serena Williams on Motherhood, Marriage, and Making Her Comeback," www.vogue.com, January 10, 2018.

TURNING THAT STD UPSIDE DOWN

American Sexual Health Organization, "Women and STIs," www.ashasexualhealth.org.

Johns Hopkins Medicine Health Library, "Oral Herpes," www.hopkinsmedicine.org.

Quest Diagnostics, "Stop STDs," www.letstalkaboutstds.com, 2017.

World Health Organization, "Globally, an estimated two-thirds of the population under 50 are infected with herpes simplex virus type 1," www.who.int, October 28, 2015.

Julie Zeilinger, "Here Are the Worst Myths About STIs According to the Women Who Have Them," www.mic.com, September 25, 2015.

YOU ARE MORE THAN YOUR TANK TOP

Meher Ahmad, "Casino Cocktail Servers Not Thrilled With Torturous High Heel Mandate," www.jezebel.com, June 11, 2013.

BBC News, "London Receptionist 'Sent Home for Not Wearing Heels,'" www.bbc.com, May 11, 2016.

Emily Blatchford, "This Is What Wearing Heels All Day Does to Your Body," www.huffingtonpost.com.au, September 18, 2016.

Natasha Burton, "One Bar's Dress Code Caused Some Serious Controversy," www.cosmopolitan.com, June 19, 2013.

Erika Harwood, "Megyn Kelly Loved Her Spaghetti-Strap RNC Dress So Much She Wore It Again," www.vanityfair.com, December 19, 2016.

Alex Heigl, "Chicago Producer Tells Female Reporters Not to Wear Hats On-Air; Says They 'Look a Lot Better Without,'" www.people.com, January 7, 2016.

Amanda Hess, "Female Lawyers Who Dress Too 'Sexy' Are Apparently a 'Huge Problem' in the Courtroom," www.slate.com, March 21, 2014.

Anthony Joseph, "And Now the 10 O'Clock Shoes! Fiona Bruce Presents BBC's Flagship Bulletin in TRAINERS as She Recovers from Breaking Her Foot," www.dailymail.co.us, May 8, 2016.

Sources

Isabelle Khoo, "Discovery Girls Magazine's Swimsuit Story Causes Outrage," www.huffingtonpost.ca, May 11, 2016.

Sierra Marquina, "Megyn Kelly Was Shamed for Wearing This Dress During the RNC—Read the Craziest Reactions," www.usmagazine.com, July 21, 2016.

Alexandra Petri, "Absurd Things That Almost Happened: Montana's Yoga Pants Ban," www.washingtonpost.com, February 12, 2015.

Daniel Politi, "Reporter Is Forced to Put on Sweater Live on Air to Cover Up 'Revealing' Dress," www.slate.com, May 15, 2016.

Jana Shortal, "I'm a TV Newswoman, and No Thanks on the Lady Uniform," www.startribune.com, June 14, 2016.

EVERYONE HAS A CHOICE...UNLESS YOU'RE A WOMAN AND IT'S BEEN TAKEN AWAY FROM YOU

Center for Public Policy Priorities, www.forabettertexas.org.

Eliza Collins and Maureen Groppe, "Donnelly One of Few Democrats to Back Anti-abortion Bill," www.indystar.com, January 29, 2018.

Tara Culp-Ressler, "Epic One-Woman Filibuster Blocks Radical Anti-Abortion Legislation In Texas," www.thinkprogress.org, June 26, 2013.

Guttmacher Institute, TRAP Laws, www.guttmacher.org.

Sarah Kliff, "10 Facts That Explain How America Regulates Abortion," www.vox.com, January 21, 2016.

Claire Landsbaum, "Arkansas Law Could Require Women to Get Their Partner's Permission for an Abortion," www.thecut.com, July 13, 2017.

NARAL, TRAP Laws, www.prochoiceamerica.com.

Linley Sanders, "Inside: The States with One Abortion Clinic: Kentucky Fights for Its Last Provider in 2018," www.newsweek.com, January 8, 2018.

Sandhya Somashekhar and Amy B. Wang, "Lawmaker Who Called Pregnant Women a 'Host' Pushes Bill Requiring Fathers to Approve Abortion," www.washingtonpost.com, February 14, 2017.

Bart Stupak, "The Case for Democrats Helping Anti-Abortion Candidates," www.time.com, August 8, 2017.

CONCLUSION

Jennifer Swan, "Why is it So Hard to Catch Drink-Drugging Assholes?" www.laweekly.com, November 16, 2016.

ABOUT THE AUTHOR

Three-time Emmy-nominated Southern loudmouth **Erin Gibson** is an expert at mixing social commentary, political satire, and vagina jokes into neat little comedy packages. Based in Los Angeles, she's one half of the *Throwing Shade* empire, which includes an award-winning political absurdist comedy podcast, international live touring show, the Funny or Die Web series, and a TV Land late-night show. She developed her social commentary chops as the host of *Modern Lady* and sharpened them writing and directing political sketches for Funny or Die, where you've seen her impersonate terrible women like Michele Bachmann, Megyn Kelly, Michelle Duggar, and Ivanka Trump. She also created the long-running Emmy-nominated *Gay of Thrones* starring her real-life hairstylist, Jonathan Van Ness, as well as the historical comedy podcast *History: The Shequel*. *Feminasty* is her debut book of comedic essays.